Walk Your Talk

Tools and Theories To Share
Nonviolent Communication

LIV LARSSON

www.friareliv.com

Published by
Friare Liv
Mjösjölidvägen 477
946 40 Svensbyn
Telefon: + 46 911- 24 11 44
info@friareliv.se
www.friareliv.com

Walk your talk, Tools and theorys to help share Nonviolent Communication © Copyright: Liv Larsson 2019.

Hoping that the contents of this book will reach as many people as possible, we encourage you to quote from this book within copyright laws. If you wish to use the contents in any other form, please contact the publisher.

Author: Liv Larsson
Translator: Katarina Hoffman and Liv Larsson
Edotor: Belinda Poropudas
Proofreader: Amy Dyer
Cover & Layout: Kay Rung
Cover picture: Istockphotos

ISBN Printed edition 978-91-87489-70-9
ISBN ePub 978-91-87489-71-6

Contents

Introduction	10
Some Ideas on How to Use This Book	11
Part 1	13
Preparing yourself	13

Chapter 1
Presentation Skills á la Nonviolent Communication (NVC) 14

Nonviolent Communication (NVC)	15
Two Assumptions That NVC is based On	15
Connecting Feelings to Needs	16
Applications of Nonviolent Communication	18
Presentation Skills á la Nonviolent Communication	19
Relating versus Performing	20
Elevator Speech	21
Listen While You Talk	22
Listen with Your Ears, Your Eyes, Your Intellect and Your Heart	23
Myths About Speaking In Front of a Group	24
My First NVC Introduction	24
Being "Perfect" - an Impossibility	26
Creating Connection	26
The foundation	28
Structures that are serving learning	31
Introduction	32
The First 5-15 Minutes	32
Involving Participants	33
Walk your Talk	36
Choosing Exercises with Care	37
Pause and Reflect	38
Play and Have Fun	38
Learning Styles	38
Repetition	39
Ideas about How to End a Workshop	40

Finish on Time 41
Summary 43

Chapter 2
Inner preparation **46**
Making Friends With Our Inner Critic 47
Inner Preparations 49
Inner preparation is as important as outer preparation 49
Quick Hints When You Feel Nervous about Leading a Group 50
Exercise – Preparing Your Inner Climate 51
If It Feels Challenging to Talk To a Group - External Stimuli 52
Expectations and Demands on Yourself 54
The Needs Behind Your Leadership 54
Your Motivation for Leading Groups? 55
What Needs Do You Want to Meet By Leading Trainings and Seminars 56
Useful reminders 57

Chapter 3
To Plan or Not To Plan, is That The Question? **58**
Checklist - Design and Content 59
The group 60
Prepare and be aware 61
Therapy or Training 67
Training Content 68
Half-day NVC-training 69
One-Day NVC-training 70
Two-day NVC-training 71
Exercises to choose from 72
 Exercises 73
The Basic Components of NVC 74
Request Circles 77
Misery Café (Jackal Café) 79
Variations Of The Exercise 81
Four choices – Four Ways of listening 83
Preparations and materials 84

Basic Empathy Skills	88
Empathy Chairs	91
Communication Cocktail	94
On the Floor	95
NVC dialogue	97
Proposed Instructions and Hints To The Participants:	97
Ideas for Deepening	99
Pitfalls:	99
Exercises In Dealing With a "No"	101
Prepare Yourself For The "No" From Someone Else	102
Practice On How To Say "No" With The Help of NVC	103
Transform Your Anger	104
Managing Your Own Anger	104
Step 1 - Preparatory	105
What Could Have Been Going On Within The Other Person?	105
Step 2 - Expressing Anger	106
The effects of labels	106
Worldviews - ideas about human beings and life	110
Evaluate = Harvest Learning	113
Evaluation	114
How Was It?	115
Evaluating Your Effort as the Trainer	116
Ending a Group That Has Been a Group During Longer Time	117
Part 2	119
Leading the group	119

Chapter 4
Dilemmas + Challenges = Nutrition for Growth 120

Dilemmas That Can Help You Grow	121
When You Do Not Get a Response	121
When someone is Talking Longer Than You (or the group) Want to Listen	123
When Someone is In Strong Need of Empathy	125
When You Get Challenging Questions	126

When you hear challenging messages	128
When you get into right-and wrong thinking	129
When Someone Ridicules what you are Talking About	131
When You Are Not Sure of Your Next Step	132
When you have inner conflicts	133
When You Find Yourself "Selling" or "Preaching"	134
When someone is Crying or Expressing Anger	136
When There Are Conflicts In the Group	136
When People Do Not Experience Their Participation as Voluntary	137
When the participants are 'talking about' rather than practicing	139
When Someone Wants to be sure of Confidentiality	140
If You are Hired Under a "False Flag"	141
When You Do Not Interrupt Although You See That It Would Make a Difference	143
Exercise - Reflections On Interrupting With Empathy	143

Chapter 5
Amongst Jackals and Giraffes - Role plays and Dialogs — 146

Jackals and Giraffes	147
What Giraffes have to do with Nonviolent Communication	147
What The Jackal Puppet and Jackal Ears Can Contribute To	149
A Jackal With Giraffe Ears	150
Role playing - some ideas of how to do it	151
As Part Of the Role play Somebody May:	153
Different types of role play	154
When the different types of role plays are useful:	155
Prepare yourself for role plays	156
Recovering from an unsuccessful role play	157

Chapter 6
Need based Leadership — 160

Leadership & Key Differentiations	162
How To "Do" Logical (realistic, clear)?	164
To Be a Human Leader	165

Motivating People	167
Goal Orientation	168
The task of the leader	169
Formal and Informal Leaders	169
The "Best" Management Style	171
The Charge of Leadership	173
The Domination System and Leadership	175
View Of Human Beings	176
The Self-fulfilling Prophecy Of The System	177
The Difference Between Systems Focusing on Domination and Systems (more directly) Focusing on Serving Life	180

Chapter 7
Need based Groups — 185

FIRO – Fundamental Interpersonal Relations Orientation	186
FIRO and NVC	187
The Inclusion Phase	187
In the Inclusion Phase the Members of the Group Often Choose to:	189
Summary Of the Inclusion Phase	190
The Control Phase	191
Vulnerable expressions	192
Summary of The Control Phase	195
Openness Phase	196
Summary Of The Openness Phase	199
Leadership in the Inclusion Phase	201
Using NVC as a Leader in The Inclusion Phase	201
Agreements and Schedule	202
The Leader can Interrupt	203
The Openhearted Leader	204
Evaluate Your Leadership in The Inclusion Phase	206
Leadership in the Control Phase	206
Using NVC as a Leader in the Control Phase	207
Handling Conflicts	211
Evaluating Your Leadership in The Control Phase	212
Leadership in Openness Phase	213

Using NVC As a Leader (Openness Phase)	213
Evaluating Your Leadership in The Openness Phase	214
Intermediate Stages	215
The Leader Helps the Group to Develop	217
When The Group is In The Phase of Comfort	218
When The Group is in Idyll Phase	218
Natural or Cultural	218
When Theories are Used as Weapons	219
Teambuilding	220
Talking About The Group Process	221
FAQ on Groups & Leadership	222

Appendix
Key Differentiations - Keys To Deepen Connection and Understanding — 227
Gaining Clarity — 227

Key Differentiations:
Key Differentiations	229
List of feeling words	236
List of words for human needs	237
Literature and references	238

Introduction

We must be the change we wish to see in the world.
Mahatma Gandhi

To be the change we want to see in the world as Gandhi is suggestion, is often a challenge. But it is also a possibility when we are sharing our understanding of Nonviolent Communication (NVC) with others. I try my best to "walk my talk," while sharing the NVC process. Modeling the NVC approach can at time be challenging but also very stimulating as it gives me continuous opportunities to learn more.

Whenever I want to dig deeper into an issue, I take the chance to share with others what I already know about the subject. To teach, be it formally in class or in a workshop, or informally, in a private conversation, tends to give the "teacher" added insights into the subject. I don't believe that you have to master a subject to be able to teach it or share it with others. What you need is a longing to share what you know and be open where you still have more to learn yourself and therefore learn along with the rest of the group.

I have written this book, hoping to provide inspiration for those wanting to share NVC in study groups or workshops. I would have liked to have had a book like this in my hand when I first began to share my understanding of NVC.

Writing this book has given me the chance to describe how I combine NVC and my experience of group-process. Read chapter 7 where I describe how FIRO (Fundamental Interpersonal Relations Orientation) can be used together with NVC to lead and understand groups and leadership. I share my view on how these two approaches can be used to support each other and this will hopefully serve as inspiration for anyone wanting to use NVC in groups.

Some Ideas on How to Use This Book

- If you want ideas on how to start a presentation, see Chapter 1, under "The First 5-15 Minutes".

- To get ideas about how to contribute to connection and how to involve your audience, see Chapter 1, under "Involving Participants" and "Creating Connection."

- If you are concerned about certain questions participants might ask, reflect on how you would like to answer them and make it the backbone of your presentation, see Chapter 4 in "When You Get Challenging Questions."

- If you are looking for exercises, topics to emphasize, and help on how to choose, there is a planning tool and a set of exercises in Chapter 3.

- If you're nervous at the thought of facing a group, you might want to practice in advance how to handle challenging situations. In that case, see Chapter 2 under the heading "Handling Internal Conflicts."

- To get more connected with what is going on within you when you are leading a group, read in particular, Chapter 3.

- If you are curious about how to built a need-based leadership, see, in particular, Chapter 7.

- To gain a deeper understanding of theoretical concepts of NVC, use the appendix on the topic of Key Differentiations.

- To develop your ability to create role plays and simulations as a learning and healing tool, see Chapter 6, "Among Jackals and Giraffes."

Part 1

Preparing yourself

Chapter 1

Presentation Skills á la Nonviolent Communication (NVC)

Nonviolent Communication (NVC)

Nonviolent Communication (NVC) can be described as a combination of thinking and communicating. It can also be described as an approach in how to use power. The aim is to create a quality of connection between people in such a way that a willingness to contribute to everyone's needs is brought to life. This means an approach in which everyone's needs are valued. Mutual respect and autonomy play a key role because they are both needed if we want to achieve effective cooperation and when we want to handle conflicts effectively.

Two Assumptions That NVC is based On

NVC is not just a way to communicate, even if it is often perceived that way. NVC is based on several assumptions and key principles. I often use the 3 assumptions below as the core of my presentations of NVC. They create clarity and strengthen my ability to handle challenging questions.

It is easier to create connection between people:

1. when we try to connect to the idea that whatever human beings do, they do it to try to meet universal needs.

2. if we assume that human beings enjoy contributing to us and others.

3. if we assume that human beings enjoy contributing if they experience it as voluntary.

Connecting Feelings to Needs

I often use the image below to describe NVC. I especially appreciate that it is circular rather than linear as this is closer to how communication works. I also like that it clearly shows that all four components of NVC are important to communication and that they are linked together.

This image illustrates – through placing "connection" in the center - that this is the main purpose of NVC. With the help of this image we can make it clear that the four components: Observation, feelings, needs, and requests often are a shorter way to connection than demands, threats, analyses and interpretations. Notice that I say "a shorter way" and not "the right way," a distinction that is important for me. Just because a person make demands or judge others it does not mean that they don't want to connect, but these ways of communication can often complicate things.

People that want to learn about NVC, usually start off with the same attitude as when they study other subjects. Most of us have learned that there is a "right" or "wrong" way to act. As NVC is less useful when it is done with that attitude, I often remind my students that there is a difference between regarding using the components of NVC as "right" than to use them as "helpful tools" in creating connection. In making that distinction, the core of NVC also gets clarified.

I want to share what I see as an effective way to communicate. However, I want to be open to the possibility that connection can be created in many different ways and that it often happens without words. Something I emphasize, when I share the NVC-process, is the importance of connecting our feelings to our needs. I sometime use the image of a tree to clarify the relation between feelings and needs.

Using the image on the next page I ask participants to associate the words that describe feelings, (which I have written on the branches), with the words for needs, (which I have written at the roots). If the word "integrity" is at the roots to describe a need, I ask, for example:

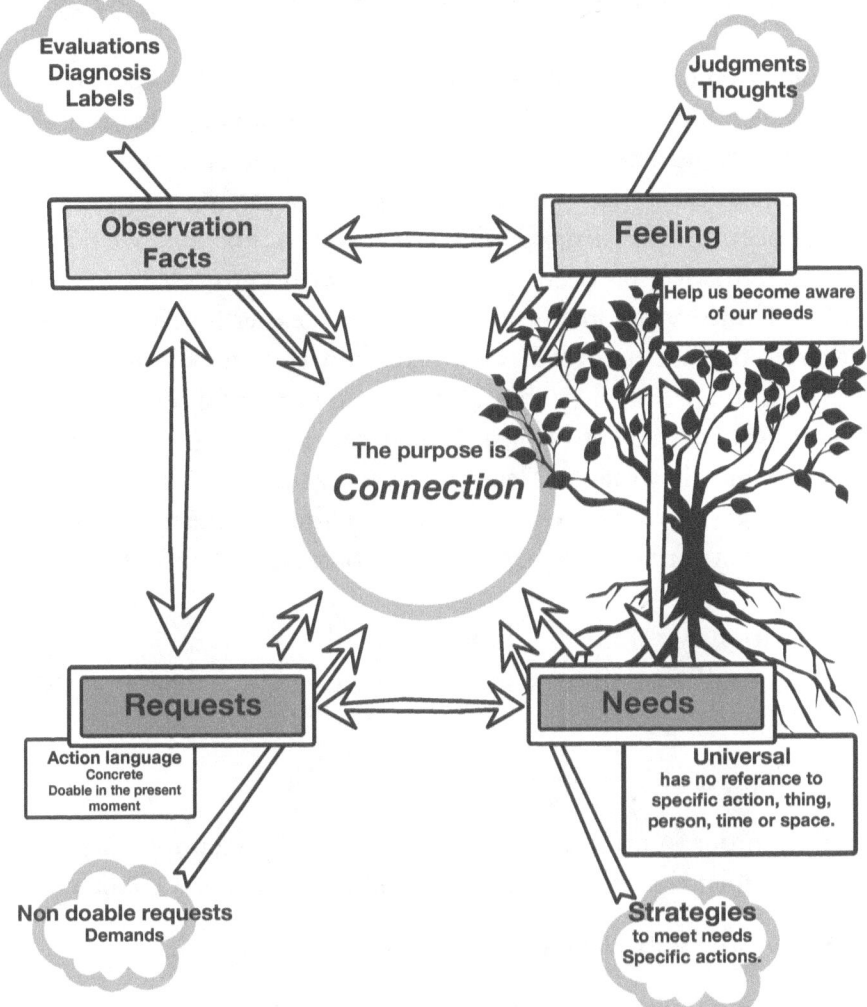

What might you feel when that need of yours is met?
or:
What might you feel when that need is not met?

I also use the tree metaphor and the link between branches and roots in the opposite direction and ask:

What needs of yours might not be met when you feel disappointed?
or:
What needs could have been met if you feel happy?

Applications of Nonviolent Communication

People often ask when to use NVC. Is it a tool to use at special moments like in conflicts? a way of speaking in everyday life or just an approach to human connection or personal development?

It is possible to use NVC in all situations where we are interested in connecting. The aim of NVC is to create connection. We do that through uncovering needs, as needs - according to NVC - are universal. Connection on a need level makes it easier for us to see each other as human beings. If your intention is to make others obey or act as you think they should, there are other and more effective ways to do that. Fear of punishment can make people do as you demand but they may not learn what you would like them to learn. In the same way a promise of a reward makes people more focused on the reward than on what they can contribute to others.

Situations where NVC skills are useful:
- In conflicts: When you are part of a conflict or act as a third party.
- In expressing appreciation and gratitude.
- In order to understand yourself better. For example, if you are torn between different choices or are facing a challenge.
- Dealing with violence and other threatening situations.
- Dealing with anger, shame and guilt.
- Strengthening connection and cooperation in families, workplaces etc.
- Connecting with people that have different opinions, religious beliefs and way of living than you.
- Influencing organizations at various levels to become more focused on meeting needs.
- Inspiring Social Change.

Presentation Skills á la Nonviolent Communication

No one knows what he can do until he tries.
Publilius Syrus, Maxims

Your heart is pounding, you are sweating and your mouth feels dry. Or maybe even worse, you have become paralyzed and cannot really feel or do anything. Something that was meant to be fun, meaningful and stimulating has turned into a nightmare. You may feel so shaky that you are sure you will forget everything you planned to share with the audience. You are not alone in finding it challenging to speak before large groups. I have met people at all levels of the "scale of nervousness."

Research shows that the thought of talking to a large group is as frightening for many as the thought of dying or the prospect of someone close to them getting seriously ill. Why? What is it that makes the thought of standing before a group so scary? Maybe one answer is that everyone is focusing on you and you do not know that they are "on your side" or some enemy to run away from?

You may not feel the slightest anxiety at the thought of speaking to a group. It might rather be a matter of feeling a little blasé and you cannot really find any passion in presenting anything. You do not know how to find motivation or get engaged. At the same feeling relaxed and being present feels impossible?

My intention is not to tell you what to say but more how to find inspiration in how to do it. I hope that you will gain strength and inspiration to:
 - dare to speak to a group of people even if you have not done so before;
 - rediscover the passion you felt earlier, but have lost for the moment;
 - help you to lead groups in a way that you are satisfied with.

Relating versus Performing

Perfectionism is not the same thing has striving to be your best. Perfectionism is the belief that if we live perfect, look perfect, and act perfect, we can minimize or avoid the pain of blame, judgment, and shame. It's a shield. It's a twenty-ton shield that we lug around thinking it will protect us when, in fact, it's the thing that's really preventing us from flight.[1]

A dilemma many of us face is that we think we have to deliver, to be good at presenting something, or to perform in a special way when we stand in front of a group. With NVC and the tools in this book I hope to inspire you to shift your focus from performing to relating. If we let go of the idea that we are standing in front of our audience to perform, and instead try to connect with them, our way of responding will demonstrate how to use the NVC-principles and thus contribute to a direct illustration. It is a golden opportunity to show them live how to deal with different opinions, to clarify misunderstandings or even deal with conflicts.

Speaking in front of a group can be as natural as eating a meal with your family and at the same time as stimulating as going for the adventure of your life. Relaxing into the connection is not about letting go of being clear or direct. You can still strive for mastery but in connection with the audience and yourself as your main focus. When we focus on relating we are one step closer to creating connection. It is about communicating in a way that is alive in the moment and being ready to connect.

When I talk about this, I am often asked what techniques and tricks I use to make this happen. Of course the experiences I have made over the years adds to the chances that I will be able to connect with others. But foremost it is about having the intention to value my relationships to others and being willing to connect to another human being. I also often use the assumption that behind everything a person says there are important human needs. Remembering that, makes it easier and more meaningful to connect

---

[1] Brown, Brené (2010) *The Gifts of Imperfection: Let Go of Who You Think You're Supposed to Be and Embrace Who You Are.* Hazelden Publishing

even with complaints or insults.

To walk your talk when it comes to NVC is to shift from performing to relating.

Elevator Speech

Imagine you are in an elevator and someone asks you the question, *What is Nonviolent Communication?*

In the short time it takes until the elevator arrives at your floor, you wish to give an answer that the other can connect to. To present what NVC is in a short time, it is useful to try to gain an understanding of what that person might need to hear to be able to know if NVC can be useful to him or her. Consider a situation you think the person has been through. Say, for example:
You know in the morning when the kids sometimes want to do everything but what you ask them to ... then proceed to explain how NVC can be used in the situation.

You know in the morning when the kids sometimes want to do anything but what you ask them to? In that situation NVC can help you connect with them and create a way to cooperate that can work for all of you.

or,
When in a work group or in a relationship, you cannot find a way to come to an agreement NVC can help you find a solution that considers everyone's needs and requests.

Practicing making elevator speeches for situations where you might get this question often helps to create clarity for yourself as well. I feel some discomfort because I'm afraid it will sound like I am suggesting some kind of "propaganda" preparation. What I want is to give concise information to people who wonder what NVC is, so that they can decide for themselves if learning NVC is for them.

Listen While You Talk

In his book *Be Heard Now,* Lee Glickstein claims that the trouble in speaking to a group is not a "talking problem" but a "listening problem."[2] He says that if we focus on and listen for signs that the participants wish to contribute and support us, there is a shift in our way of relating to them. He emphasizes the importance of listening before we speak, as we speak, and when we have stopped speaking. When we listen the way Glickstein suggests, it becomes easier to determine whether we could benefit from slowing down, taking a break, asking something or doing something else that contributes to more connection with the participants.

I suggest that you speak about NVC (or whatever you're talking about) to a group in the same way as in a personal conversation with a single individual; for a start you connect with the other person in order to know what she or he wants from you. Connection with a group is based on the same principle. That is; you listen to the participants and express what is going on in you. Being open with what is going on in you is equally important as listening.

Although it might sound impossible to listen as we are speaking to a group - it can be done simultaneously. We listen to body language, gestures and words and we show that we are ready to take in what is communicated to us.

When we listen to others, it is more likely that they will want to listen to us. It does not matter whether it's just one individual, or a person in a group. Everyone wants to be heard and taken seriously.

It is also important to be able to handle silence and to have the courage to stay connected as well when no words are used. I am not talking about taking a rhetorical pause used as a technique for increasing interest in something particular. I am talking about the kind of silence that can occur when we connect, human to human.

It is not up to us to resolve our listeners' frustration or confusion. We do give them our attention and answer their questions. We invite them to speak up and we listen to them, whatever it is, that is of importance for them to express. We also might ask someone

---

2. Glickstein, Lee (1999), *Tap Into Your Inner Speaker and Communicate With Ease.* Broadway books.

to bring this up with us in person afterwards, if we assess that the matter that they are bringing up is not contributing to the group.

Listen with Your Ears, Your Eyes, Your Intellect and Your Heart

Talking about "learning to listen" might be misleading. It is all about being willing to give someone our full attention; to "listen with our heart," to just be there without any particular agenda. What we might learn is how to focus our attention. For example when we use the tools we have in NVC, we primarily listen for the needs and feelings of others and what they value and dream of. We might use words when listening, to support the person we are listening to, to find words to express themselves and what they are feeling and needing. We might also use words to show others that we are really trying to understand what they want us to hear by reflecting back what we are hearing. This way of listening not only helps others to be more present, it also helps us to be "here and now."

When we express what is going on in us – in order to make it easier to connect - we also try to use words in a way that makes it as easy as possible for others to hear us compassionately. It is usually easier to listen to us with empathy if we talk about ourselves and what we need, rather than on making analysis of the other person.

When speaking before groups, many of us are focused on what is going on within us. Our heart is pounding, our legs are shaking and we are analyzing all possible ways of how we are perceived. Perhaps we become occupied with trying either to calm ourselves down or on finding ways to hide our nervousness. If we instead focus on how to connect it will result in quite a different kind of presence.[3]

---

[3]. For more inspiration, read Glickstein, Lee (1999), *Be Heard Now! Tap Into Your Inner Speaker and Communicate With Ease*. Broadway books.

Myths About Speaking In Front of a Group

The first two myths are taken from Lee Glicksteins excellent book, *Be Heard Now! Tap Into your inner speaker and communicate with ease* where he also gives more examples of strong beliefs when it comes to performance. The third one is an abbreviation.

Myth #1: Public speaking is about mastering performance and winning the audience over with style and technique.

My proposal: If we express what is "alive" within us, it will help us connect to our audience. If we are also willing to show that we are capable of either taking care of ourselves or ask for support it will help the presentation.

Myth #2: Stage fright must be conquered and overcome.

My proposal: Stage fright can be managed by creating connection with what you feel, and then to link it to what you need and finding a way to meet the needs. You need to honor it to be able to move through it

Myth 3: I need to be funny and make people laugh.

My proposal: People are happy to laugh when they feel free to do so. People like to have fun and they laugh more when they are relaxed and supported.

My First NVC Introduction

I often – half in jest – say that my first NVC introduction was the best presentation I ever made. The reason for this is that I was nervous and at the same time totally honest about my nervousness and took responsibility for it.

Since NVC was the theme of the introduction, I used my feelings and immediately talked about and modeled some essential parts of NVC. I told the audience this was the first time I was speaking before a group about NVC. As NVC – and its effects on me - had become more and more valuable to me, sharing it was quite a vulnerable experience for me. I told them about my vulnerability and fear of not being received in this situation that was so important to me. I told the group that I was nervous about not having enough clarity to be able to show them what I found most valuable with the NVC process, but that I was willing to have a go at it anyway.

In hindsight I think the fact that I quickly showed my humanity created a connection that made the conversation flow. This made the rest of the workshop relaxed and fun. I realized (afterwards) that I managed to balance my connection with my inner self, my own nervousness and the connection with the participants. As a start I said something like this:

I feel nervous standing here and at the same time I am enjoying it a lot. I am enjoying it because what I am going to share is so valuable for me. And I am nervous because I do not know if I will be able to be as clear as I would like to be. Something that would be supportive for me and also help me get more connected with you is to hear from three or four of you, about what you would like to learn about communication. Is there someone who would like to say something about this?

After having heard some requests from different people and responding to them, I continued:

What I want to share with you is my understanding of NVC. I am inspired by Marshall Rosenberg and what I am going to share with you is my interpretation and understanding of what he calls NVC.

After this introduction, I experienced a strong connection with the group and with myself. It made me feel calmer and more secure in a way I would never have been, had I tried to "pretend" that I was not nervous. My honesty about my nervousness and about my need for connection and safety paved the way for connection during the workshop.

Being "Perfect" - an Impossibility

Leading a group studying NVC is not about being able to answer all the questions about everything concerning communication. It's more about the courage to be vulnerable and honest about what is going on in you, with a willingness to listen to what is going on in others. Practicing how our language can be used, in as many situations as possible – and not just "talking about it" – is usually more rewarding for the participants.

If I show that I'm willing to take responsibility for what I feel by connecting my feelings to my needs, my openness will build confidence and security for the whole group. This is in contrast to just telling them that I feel nervous - without showing that I am also capable of taking care of these feelings - which often leads to the participants also getting nervous or becoming unfocused.

Of course it helps to be well prepared; especially if we are not comfortable with being open about what is going on within us. Some people find the basic assumptions in NVC rather provocative. Therefore, you will probably encounter some questioning when you talk about NVC. It is a major and stimulating challenge to hear their reactions with empathy, without getting defensive. I often welcome this challenge as it gives me a chance to show how I can use NVC to create connection, even with people whose opinions differ from mine.

Creating Connection

No matter whether it's NVC or anything else I want to present, first of all I want to create connection. Listening with empathy and expressing oneself with vulnerable honesty is the basis for establishing connection. Since the purpose of NVC is to communicate in a way that establishes connection, sharing NVC with a group is an opportunity to "live the process" and not just talk about it. If from the beginning you show that you want to listen to everyone's needs, it is a way to demonstrate the core of what you want to share. Showing that you are willing to try to "walk your talk" will probably make it more interesting for others to consider learning the process you are presenting.

NVC is not about trying to be perfect. One part of NVC is about mourning when you have done something that did not meet your (or someone else's) needs. This is important to reflect on, especially if you notice that your motivation for continuing to share NVC lessens if you have not been completely happy about a presentation or a training.

The connection between you and the "participants" sends a message that is just as important as the words you speak. When others see that you are willing to create connection with people in the group, it will probably contribute to their trust in your willingness to see them as humans. This is valuable to remember, especially if we are facing a large group and have been taught that we should try to look at everyone's face, as a technique for making everyone feel seen. Focus on connecting rather than on using a certain technique. Once we have found our "smallest common denominator"; our humanity, our needs, it will become easier to connect. If we focus on what we all have in common, compassion is brought about – as we recognize each other's similarities. And when compassion is established I have great confidence that it is possible to create and maintain connection. It is not about adopting someone's viewpoint or giving up on something you believe in – it is about connecting on the level of needs.

Here are some of the questions about connection you may ask yourself prior to a presentation:

How can I contribute to the connection between me and the participants?

How can I ask for the support I need in order to contribute to connection?

How can I help the participants to create connection with each other?

How can I support the quality of connection that makes it easy for everyone's needs to be heard?

The foundation

There are different reasons for why we feel inspired to share something with others. In order to present a topic it is helpful to have some kind of foundation to build on. And to know which "building block" is it especially important for you to describe in depth.

I usually express my basic assumptions in order to make it easier for others to capture why I am saying what I am saying. People usually feel safer in asking questions if they know my underlying assumptions. At the same time, by expressing my assumptions I find it easier to relax. It also reminds me of my focus and my longing to share what is helpful for me.

When my "building blocks" are known, for example my assumptions about "human nature," it gives the people listening a reference point for where they themselves stand. Hopefully they start reflecting upon their own assumptions about human nature, and do not feel compelled to make on the same ones as I do.

If throughout the presentation I come back to my original assumptions it is easier for the participants to follow and understand what I mean and what I want to share, and why.

One basic assumption I often use as a starting point when introducing NVC is:

I find it is easier to understand others if I focus on the idea that behind every action a human being does there are some needs that they are trying to meet.

Put into words, whatever assumption you want to present, preferably in one sentence or two to make it easier for the participants to remember. Write it on a flip chart or hand out in advance. Use an assumption that is in accordance with your values and beliefs. Return to it as often as you can to create clarity for the listeners.

Opening up for the participants to express something or ask questions at the beginning of a seminar or workshop often contributes to connection. I want to make clear that one of my assumptions is that we have the same basic needs, and that their engagement is of help to meet my need for community. This can be done in many different ways. However it is important to pay attention to the fact that for many people deep human contact can be a vulnerable experience. Some may be shy or embarrassed about coming closer than expected to others. This is not surprising! Connecting deeply with someone, often throws a different light on what is going on within us and therefore we easily feel exposed and vulnerable.

Connection is a universal need and when it is met it is most often perceived as extremely meaningful and life giving. Once we dare to take the step to get closer to someone else, connection may seem like the safest place in the world.

In small groups:
Invite the group into a circle, where you ask everyone to say his or her name and what they want to learn about this subject and why.

In larger groups:
Start by saying that you want some understanding of what has motivated them to participate and that you would like to hear from two or three participants.

I would like to understand more about why you have come to this workshop. It is not possible right now to hear everyone's reasons, but I would like to hear from at least two or three of you. Is anyone willing to tell me what motivated you to come here?

Some people are shy of talking in larger groups, and some people may hesitate to express themselves for other reasons. Before making the request in the large group, you can ask the participants to pair up and talk to each other about why they have come to your workshop, what they are interested in and what they want to learn. When the participants have "warmed up" this way and expressed themselves to one another, it may be easier for them to say something in front of the rest of the group as well.

If in spite of this no one wants to speak up in front of the group, you can express your feelings and needs in that very moment and make a new request. Make a fresh start by meeting their silence with a compassionate guess. It may sound like this:

> *It might be rather hard to figure out what you want to know about this before I have even started, right?*
>
> or,
>
> *Perhaps you are feeling a little nervous and would like to feel safer before you say something?*

Many times, it is supportive for those who are nervous and reluctant to talk, if you try to put yourself in their situation. The way they are sitting can influence whether people will talk or not. If chairs are placed, for example in rows, in such a way that everyone is looking at you, they do not see each other's faces which complicates their interaction. Many people become quiet when they sit like that, simply because it does not feel safe. It might also remind them of their schooldays, where they were supposed to behave and speak only when asked to do so. You will find more about this under the heading "How to be seated" on page 64.

When an authority makes requests, others often perceive them as demands. This applies especially to requests made by authorities that are in power, such as managers or teachers. If you hear something as a demand it is easy to rebel, submit or become silent. Most of us have experienced, when asked a question by a teachers that it was about answering correctly or saying something that sounded smart. Such memories will, of course, reduce people's willingness to be open, especially in a group where they not yet know the others. If we ask questions that can only be answered in one way, or with a yes or a no, they can be perceived as demands and thus lead to silence.

Please, in order to maximize your chances of getting a response read more about asking under "When you do not get a response," page 121. You can also prepare questions that participants can discuss in pairs or in small groups. This might help them feel more involved and also tends to make it easier to share in the large group afterwards.

Examples of questions to ask when introducing NVC:
"What can create connection between people?"
"What gets in the way of human connection?"
"Whose responsibility is it to communicate effectively?"
"Do you have some specific challenges in terms of communication?"
"What happens to your communication if you feel guilty, or think that you have done something wrong or if you hear criticism?" *"Think of an experience when you felt fully present while listening to someone. How did it feel? What made that possible?"*
"Have you ever felt that you were really understood? What allowed that to happen?"

Structures that are serving learning

It will be helpful for the participants, in a seminar or training if you already, when introducing yourself, clearly tell something about your values and what you want to convey to them. Lee Glickstein says that an audience wants to have answers to four burning questions when they listen to someone.[4]

Answering these fours questions with a personal story can help those involved connect to you as they get your answers.

1.Who are you?
Glickstein suggests that we respond to that question by telling a short personal history that has meaning for both you and the audience. Talk briefly about something that you used to regard as challenging, but now can handle. I often start by telling how I used to quarrel with my dad and how I through NVC found a way to create a deep and meaningful connection with him during his last years.

At other times I have started by talking about how my partner and I did not understand each other and how it led to some bushes in our garden being - unintentionally - cut down. I use the story to illustrate how counterproductive it is to look for whose fault some-

---
[4]. For more inspiration read Glickstein, Lee (1999), Tap Into Your Inner Speaker and Communicate With Ease. Broadway books.

thing is when we want to connect.

2. Why are you here? Why are you talking about this?
Here, I share my experience and how I'm helped by what I'm sharing.

3. What will we do? What will the participants be asked to do – just listen, be part of some exercises etc.?
You can answer this question by using three or four sentences describing your idea of how you would like to spend your time together.

4. What can I get out of this?
Talk about the expectations the listeners might have about your presentation. Tell them what you think they can get out of your time together. Also consider if there is something in particular you want to say about yourself that you think might be useful for them to know and to connect to. If the audience consists of dentists you can, for example, tell about how you have benefited from the dentists in your life. In pointing out the fact that you are a human being beyond your role in this training or seminar, might make it easier for them to connect to you.

Introduction - The First 5-15 Minutes

Take your time; just stand or sit in front of the group, preferably at least one minute, maybe longer, before you start talking. Let the participants 'study' you. Make eye contact with some people and talk to someone in the audience. Preferably someone you do not know. Focus on creating contact and "showing your humanness" i.e. availability, that you are there for them and with them. Express your feelings in the moment and what needs they are based on. Demonstrate that you know how to handle your feelings by taking responsibility for them and attribute them to your needs.

In workshops on public speaking and how to facilitate groups you might have been taught that one should not talk about or show nervousness, as it is uncomfortable for the participants if the facilitator is anxious and nervous. What may be hard for the listeners are the strategies some facilitators use, trying to hide their nervousness. The strategies vary, but pretending that we feel something we are not feeling usually stimulates insecurity, frustration, or confusion in others.

My experience is that it is not uncomfortable to hear the speaker expressing that she is nervous if she is also able to show that she is able to take care of it herself.

Tell the audience what you plan to cover and talk about and what needs of yours are met by your doing so. Clarify what motivates you to share what you want to share. This will help people find their own idea of why this could be an important subject. Depending on what you are feeling and needing in that moment, it might sound like this:

I feel happy and at the same time a bit nervous to be here. I'm happy because the process I want to share with you is so valuable to me. I'm also nervous, as it's exciting to see how I will manage to share this stuff - that is so important to me – with you.

Involving the Participants

When you share NVC, I recommend that you invite the participants to practice each component separately. If the different parts of the process are clear, it contributes to the understanding of the whole. This is a great opportunity for the participants to interact. It also gives them the opportunity to apply and anchor NVC in situations from their own lives to such an extent, as they want to.

Feelings:
More Exercises around feelings can be found in "Connecting feelings to needs," page 16. Here are a few:
 - Ask the participants to share their responses to the two questions below. Then use their responses to either talk about the next step in the model or to practice a situation of their choice:

How does it feel to communicate or spend time with people who do not express their feelings?

If you could choose to be born with or without feelings, what would you choose and why?

- Ask the participants to put into words what they feel right now (either in pairs or in the whole group). This may contribute to learning and at the same time create connection. In many situations people experience vulnerability when being open about their feelings. (See below.) Therefore, I use this exercise in a playful way, more as a game than as a matter of exploration of deep feelings.

Once you have found words to describe feelings, you may connect those feelings to needs, be it your or someone else's feelings and needs. The participants may also react differently to people having strong, unvoiced feelings. There are many methods to work with becoming more skilled at this. For example, you can use cards showing words for feelings and needs and use them in different ways. You can also use the image of the tree as it is described on page 17.

Needs:
- Ask participants to express what needs they wanted to meet by participating in the workshop or seminar. You may then ask them to tell the group if their needs have been met so far. Their answers can provide information valuable for your development as a facilitator, as well as contribute to the participants' knowledge of needs. These are challenging questions in some contexts, so be open to different responses to what you might call needs.
- Ask participants to write a list of human needs.
- Tell the group some short stories and ask participants to guess which needs the persons in the stories have tried to meet.
- Ask them to share some judgments that they find difficult to turn into needs. Then try together to guess what the needs are and how they can be met.
- Use the image of the three on page 17.
- Use cards with words for feelings and needs in exercises and games to get more clarity.

Requests:
There are many ways to practice expressing requests, so have some fun and try different ways. Among other things you can:
- Ask if anyone has a request they want to express right now - to you or to anyone else. Help the person to make it a doable request in the present.
- Express a request of some kind and ask the group to distinguish between a request that is doable and one that is not. Express another request and ask them to distinguish whether it is a request or a demand and to clarify what the difference is.
- Choose one need and ask them to find different strategies and requests that would meet that need. Do the same with as many needs that seems fun and learning.

Write down examples of clear, doable present requests you can make to a group in different situations. It can help you demonstrate how requests may support group members to progress in a situation that would otherwise cause conflict or dissatisfaction. Make sure that these requests are specific and doable and possible to act on in the present so that participants also get some inspirational examples.

Here is one request you can make when you want to invite the participants to take active part and at the same time demonstrate how requests are expressed with the help of NVC.

I'm a bit worried if what I have talked about so far has been clear and I would really like to be clear. It would help me to hear from at least three of you about what you have understood about this concept. Is anyone willing to say something about that?

Observations:
Talking about the difference between observations and evaluations works well in most groups. Many times, it is a topic not as sensitive and vulnerable as feelings and needs. I therefore sometimes choose to start with focusing on observations, hoping that more of the participants will take part in the discussions.

- Express an evaluation or judgment and ask them to decide

whether it is an observation or an evaluation and what makes it an evaluation. You might write down some examples on a flip-chart and ask the participants to work together in pairs to discuss your examples.

- Ask the participants to discuss in what way it may be useful to distinguish an observation from an evaluation if you want to connect.

- Ask the participants to recall some frequently used evaluations or judgments - for example, lazy, smart or handsome - and then ask everyone to reflect on what the person saying it may have observed.

- Ask the participants to recall some challenging label or judgment they have heard about themselves or somebody else. Ask them to work together in pairs and suggest observations that could have prompted the evaluation.

Walk your Talk

Nonviolent Communication is so much more than a theory to be mastered. It is something to be lived and used, rather than to only be talked about. NVC contain some very practical principles and tools that can be used in all communication between humans. These tools can be practiced and honed but they are not the goal. Connection is the goal. Most of the parameters in an interaction can only be guessed at beforehand. Every moment of connection has parts that are unique and that is what makes it challenging but also fun and alive. Learning NVC is learning to "dance this dance".

As a trainer, take every chance you get to demonstrate "how to live" the NVC process: i.e. when people ask questions; when decisions about breaks are made; when you decide how to place the chairs; when discussing whether microphones are needed; when talking about cell phones and how to use or not use them); or anything else that is alive in this particular group. Those situations provide opportunities to demonstrate how to take everyone's needs into account before arriving at a strategy. I regularly receive feedback from workshop participants about how helpful it has been for their understanding of NVC to experience how different desires can be managed by using this process. When you show how to use NVC, explain that you intend to use the principles and the process, and then clarify what you are doing, step by step. For example:

Now, I'm expressing a request to get information about your preferences concerning breaks. I do this to get the process forward and still consider everyones needs.

or

Now I'm reflecting back what I heard this person say, as a way to make sure she has been understood the way she wanted to.

Choosing Exercises with Care

Sometimes you are asked to introduce NVC in a workplace where the employees have been told to participate. They have not decided themselves to explore NVC. If that is the case I suggest that you are aware that the exercises you use when the participants take part out of free will may be much too self-effacing for an involuntary audience.

Choose exercises and examples that are primarily about clarifying basic aspects of NVC. If you do so it is more likely that the "non-volunteers" will choose to participate actively as they feel confident not to be asked to expose themselves more than they want to. A variety of such exercises can be found in Chapter 3 - "Exercises; the basic components of NVC" page 58.

If a participant on his or her own initiative presents a personal example it is quite another matter than if you ask them or encourage them to do so.

Pause and Reflect

Take some moments to ask the participants to pair up and share how they are affected by what you have said and how they can use this in their lives.

To repeat and share ones understanding of what one has heard makes it easier to remember. Repetition is also a way to process information to find out if it is or may become useful. To listen to how another person has received the information further broadens the understanding of the topic.

Play and Have Fun

With the words "play" and "fun" you may think that I am encouraging you to make puns and crack jokes. That's not my intention. Instead I want you to talk using personal experiences that you have found humorous and which might be of value for others to reflect on. Laugh at yourself and your mistakes, without being ironic or patronizing. This kind of "fun" comes naturally when there is connection. And the laughter lends zest to the conversation.

Let people laugh with you, give them time to laugh. Take a break when you have said something that can be humorous to others. I usually remind myself that people like to have fun and it helps me to relax and have more fun myself. There is a lot of research showing that laughter contributes to our learning.

Learning Styles

We learn 10% of what we read, 20% of what we hear, 30% of what we see, 50% of what we see and hear, 70% of what we say and 90% of what we say and do.
Vernon A Magnesen[5]

It's easy to believe that everyone takes in information and learns in the same way as we do ourselves. The result is often that we teach

5 Vos & Dryden (2005) *The New Learning Revolution.* Network Educational Press Ltd

the same way as we learn. But we all learn in different ways. This makes it an extra interesting challenge to share knowledge, information and experience with others. When you facilitate learning, try to adapt what you teach into as many learning styles as possible. It's much more than that different ways of teaching serve different learning styles. When we learn one thing in many different ways – by different senses - seeing, hearing, feeling, trying, discussing and so on, the knowledge becomes anchored. To see the same thing from different angles gives clarity to the overall picture. To "talk about" something can create clarity and trust that the process might be useful. Practicing using the knowledge is building communication skills. To learn NVC both of these are of help.

When we have been moved by what we have learned both on an emotional level and with our senses, things seem to be easier to remember and understand. We learn, among other things by hearing, seeing, touching, trying, talking and relating to others. When we share NVC, it is enjoyable and stimulating to find different ways of doing it.

Repetition

Repetition is a very useful tool when you really want to learn something. In order to anchor new knowledge it might therefore be beneficial to repeat the same or similar exercises and theories several times. It also gives participants a chance to evaluate what they have learned and to celebrate their successes.

Here are some suggestions of how to create repetition in a meaningful way:
- Divide the group into smaller groups with the task to share, for example, how they have understood the difference between observations and interpretations, emotions and thoughts and so on.
- At the end of a presentation, have each person write 5-10 questions about the content of your presentation. Then divide the participants into pairs and let them ask and answer each other's questions.

- Divide the group into pairs and let each person tell the other about, for instance, what they have experienced that was:

 - The most interesting so far,
 - The most challenging and difficult up to now,
 - The most useful thing so far.

Ideas about How to End a Workshop

The last part of a seminar or workshop is very important because it affects what people feel when they leave and what they take away. I do not usually end with a question and answer session (Q&A). From the start I make it clear that I will not have this formal question and answer session at the end. I tell the participants that I would rather hear questions whenever they come up. I prefer to see people involved and active throughout the session instead of keeping their questions to themselves until the last moment. In that way I usually have time to immediately clarify if something I said was not that clear. This is, of course, a matter of taste, so go for whatever you prefer.

Another reason I do not leave the Q&A to the end is that there may come up issues that take longer to answer than there is time for. This easily leads to your entire presentation being experienced as unfinished and parts of it being questioned just because you have not had the time to come to a mutual understanding. I help the participants make their questions by regularly asking if they have any.

Ask them to sit in pairs for a few minutes and talk about what they have learned so far. Then ask if someone wants to share their learning with the whole group. This functions as a brief repetition, brings a sense of completion and offers an (important) opportunity for people to express gratitude and give something back to others who have contributed to them. If you want to know what the participants have picked up, you can find out by simply asking:

I would like to hear from as many as possible what you have learned today that you think you will find useful in the future. Is there anyone who is willing to share?

or
Since we do not have enough time to hear from everyone, I would like to hear from at least three of you about what learning you've found most useful today?

In a smaller group, you can make a closing round and ask everyone to say something. For example:
What needs of yours have been met by this presentation?

or
Which of your needs, if any, have not been met?

Another way to end is to ask the participants to share what they have picked up that is especially important to them. Give them the space to say whatever they want to say.
- Ask the participants to share if there is something you have said or done that contributed to them in a special way.
- Ask the participants to tell if they have found something that they would like to practice more during the workshop.

Read more on ending a group under "Ending a Group That Has Been a Group During Longer Time" on page 117.

Finish on Time

The importance of keeping agreements about time differs widely from culture to culture, group to group and country to country. I usually aim to finish (and start) on time. If despite that I run over time, I ask those involved if there is anyone who minds running over by x minutes. Even if you make this as a request, it may be a challenge for some people to say so, depending for example on how well you know each other or if they see you as their teacher or boss.
I notice that there are some things I still want to say and it will take about 10 minutes longer than scheduled. I wonder if there is anyone who is not ok with staying ten more minutes and wants to leave now?
or

We will continue for 10 minutes more. I want to hear if there is anyone who needs to leave right now?

No matter how interested a person is, if they have other things on their mind - like picking up children from the day-care center, catching a bus or train or some other important activity – they will probably stop listening to you. So think twice before suggesting that you would like to finish later than agreed on.

At the beginning of a workshop, seminar or presentation, it is important to make sure that everyone has the same information about the schedule. It is also important that you make your intention to stick to the schedule known. If someone has a tight individual calendar, it's nice for them to hear this and it will help them to be more present.

The importance of keeping to the agreed time varies from country to country, but also from individual to individual and organization to organization. In Sweden, where I live, I have discovered there is almost always someone in a group who will be disturbed if I do not stick to the scheduled finishing time. In other countries where I have led trainings, for example in Poland, Estonia and Thailand, this might not be a big deal. Make sure that you do whatever you do to serve the group and yourself, and not because it is "right" to do so. Be aware that even if you are teaching in a country where time agreement is not as "holy" as in Sweden, there might be individuals that are very disturbed about not keeping to them.

Summary

- Prepare questions that will enhance connection and engagement.

- Prepare yourself for questions from the participants that might stimulate a strong emotional reaction in you.

- When asking questions - express why you want to hear something from the group (your needs).

- When expressing specific questions / requests – say what you want to hear, and from how many.

- If you tell the group what you feel, follow up directly by also saying which of your needs is at the root of your feeling.

- If you express your needs, follow them up with requests.

- If you are worried prior to a workshop or presentation - ask someone you trust to listen to you with empathy in advance.

- Do not start speaking too soon, wait for the "right" moment and let the participants settle down. Use the moment to create quiet connection with at least one of them.

- Give the audience some time to "study you." Remind yourself that they are doing so in order to meet needs.

- Take some time to ease off just before you start talking to connect with yourself.

- Show your humanity as soon as possible to facilitate connection.

- Do not apologize if you are tired or out of form. Instead you can honestly express your needs in the moment and take responsibility for what you want to do about it.

- Do not speak badly about yourself or what you are going to talk about, but share your own experiences, for example, what mistakes you have made and the difficulties you have encountered.

- Say that you are open for questions (if you are), challenges or other contributions.

- Do not tease or mock the audience, avoid being ironical, but allow yourself to be humorous about yourself.

- Take every chance to "live the process."

- Let people laugh with you, and, give them time to laugh.

- Ask yourself - what can create connection right now?

- Do not talk to but with people.

- Remind yourself that if you feel nervous, it is because some of your needs are not being met.

- Practice the worst situations you can imagine happening. Imagine how others might respond and practice creating connection.

- Spend more time preparing HOW you want to say and do things, rather than WHAT you will say.

- Do not talk faster than anyone can listen to and do not give more information than anyone can take in.

Chapter 2

Inner preparation

Making Friends With Our Inner Critic

Inward Connection, Outward Connection
Connection is everything!
Lee Glickstein[1]

We can prepare a lot to help us in giving a presentation. And it is as important to prepare on the inside as it is to prepare ourselves for actually presenting the material. An inner connection helps us connect with others, even under pressing circumstances.

Having the biggest part of our focus on creating connection with participants helps us not only in giving information, but also helps to inspire people to learn. Some people become anxious when I suggest this, saying they could never focus on this so much because then they would forget what they were going to say. However, I believe that we can trust in our knowledge, if we just find a way to relax. In a relaxed state, the information I need is more available to me than when I'm stressed. And I can rely that the information about communication will become even clearer as I connect with others.

In my preparation I also make sure I find inner connection. To talk *with*, rather than talking *at* those who listen to you, is important because it is within this connection between you that they will learn and to be able to do that inner connection is a big help.

The more connected I am with the people I'm talking with, the more able I am to use real examples of what is happening at the moment between us, and the easier it seems for people to learn. This occurs even around messy happenings, or with subjects that are not really interesting to everyone. We are able to create real learning from these moments of connection. Being connected help you to get across what you want to share.

Sharing knowledge about NVC differs in some ways from teaching about other things. It is an opportunity, to develop your ability to stay connected with yourself, even in a situation where it feels challenging to do so. I had been a trainer and consultant for

---
1. Glickstein, Lee (1999), Be Heard Now! Tap into your inner speaker and communicate with ease. Broadway books.

many years before I started sharing NVC. Although I felt nervous the first time I introduced the basics of NVC, it was a great support that I had a language with which to express my feelings and needs.

If we are "present" it can help others to be more present. People need to experience presence in order to learn about empathic listening, which is such a big part of NVC. If they just want information, they could just as easily read a book. When teaching NVC, however, we have a chance to teach by modeling what we want others to learn, rather then by just telling them about a different way to express themselves or listening.

An approach that helps me feel more relaxed is the idea that people participating in a training or workshop want to have both an enjoyable and meaningful time. Therefore, the well being of the leader is of great importance. When I remember to think in this way I feel support from the audience and therefore am also more present.

Lee Glickstein claims that "the best technique is no technique." It is easier to "be ourselves" when we let ourselves relax, to pause a moment, to take a moment of silence when we have said something that affects us. It's not the kind of silence that is based on techniques, telling you to take short breaks now and then in order to amplify your message. It is about allowing oneself to take a pause when it is most needed. Using a moment to strengthen connection within yourself and with those you are speaking with, and giving them the same opportunity, can be short, but very valuable, for the rest of the seminar, training or talk. It is not about making myself smaller or looking for where I am weak, nervous or not capable. It is about showing what is alive in me at the very moment and that might differ widely from time to time. It is about showing the part of me that others can connect to and handle.

When we trust that showing up as a human being is enough, we can drop the idea about saying "smart things". We just try to show up in an authentic way. It is seldom that the words I use make the biggest difference for people. Rather most participants express appreciation for the connection they experience and how it is created through our communication.

Inner Preparations

It is not the crime, it's the cover-up
Richard Nixon, during the Watergate Scandal

It is not our nervousness that is most distracting to those we are talking with; it is our efforts to try and hide our nervousness. When we do not try to hide anything, it's easier for others to trust what we are saying. Our attempt to hide our feelings often catches people's attention. So instead of focusing on listening to what we have to say, they are wondering about what is really going on inside of us.

If we instead express that we are nervous, and why, it usually makes it easier for others to see us as human. They can see that we are willing to be both open about what is going on within us and that we are capable of taking responsibility for it. When they trust that we are capable of taking care of even our nervousness, it makes it easier for them to focus on the content of what we are saying.

Inner preparation - as important as outer

It is useful to practice accepting the nervousness or performance anxiety you may have, no matter what emotions they are carrying. To give oneself time to embrace what is going on and to connect with what we feel about what we need, makes it more possible to talk directly "from the heart." You can practice it on your own, for example, through exercises in this chapter or with the support of others.

I often arrange to be heard with empathy by someone else just before I lead a seminar or training. It gives me the freedom to let go of anything that I might otherwise try to hide from the group or even from myself. Using the listener's ears and heart, I sort out what is going on inside of me to get more in touch with what's important to me in the moment. I let my judgments out – the ones I have about myself and the ones I have about the group that I'm about to connect to. It does not matter if they are positive or negative judgments – it is more a matter of clarity about what is going on inside of me that might get in the way of me connecting with the people I'm about to meet.

Knowing I can receive empathy while leading trainings has been a big support for me, especially when leading training was still new to me. By this "empathy support" I mean a person or people whom I know are available to me if I need immediate support. They might be at the same place as me or I can call them to listen to me as I share some challenge.

When I call them, I want to be sure they are prepared to listen to me sharing judgments about me or the participants and that they know that this is just (tragic) expressions for needs. I might also share thoughts on how I or anyone else *should* behave that I'm stuck on. What I want them to do then is just to help me find what I feel and need behind all this with empathic guesses. Sometimes even a minute of connection with them, is enough for me to find empathy and willingness to connect with myself and the group again. On some occasions I might also ask for advice but then it is usually after being received with empathy.

When You Feel Nervous about Leading a Group - Hints

- Remind yourself that if you feel nervous, you can use it to connect with some need of yours. Make sure to give space or connect with those needs.

- Remind yourself that there are many different ways to meet needs. The fact that you feel nervous says nothing about your ability to carry through with the presentation. To feel nervous will make you more alert and might even help you in being able to focus.

- Try using the approach that "we are never afraid of the reactions of another, we are afraid of how we will be able to manage how those reactions affect us." Pay attention to your own reactions, as they are what you can alter.

- Remind yourself that the response you get from others will depend on how they have listened to you. You can change what you say but not how others hear you.

- Remind yourself that it is not your nervousness that will distract people. You want to show what you feel but also that you are able to take care of those feeling.

Exercise – Preparing Your Inner Climate

This is an exercise on how to manage emotions if the stimuli exist within you. With an inner stimulus I mean thoughts, feelings, enemy images of yourself or others and so on. You might, for example, feel separated, cut-off, bored.

Use the exercise when it becomes a challenge for you to handle thoughts that bring up more emotions than what you can manage at the moment or when you feel stress in a way that gets in the way of clarity. Do the exercise well ahead of a presentation or workshop, so you have time to digest what you find out about yourself.

1. Write down the thoughts that stimulate your feeling of insecurity, fear, boredom, nervousness or numbness. Catch as many of the challenging thoughts as possible.

   (At the beginning revealing these thoughts might increase your sense of nervousness, so if it is very close to your first presentation make sure you go easy on yourself. It might be better to do this exercise in a less charged situation and go for some other kind of support. Give it time.)

2. What trigger these thoughts? Take some time at every disturbing thought so that you can really catch what stimulates them? What do you see or hear?

Even if you might claim that this is only on the inside, many times there are also outside triggers like hearing some sounds, or seeing some image that starts it off? What happened specifically at the moment when the thoughts came?

3. What feelings and needs are trying to get your attention? What do you feel when you connect to the observations (2) that are stimulating your thoughts and what needs are those feelings pointing at? Take time to get a deeper connection with your feelings and needs.

4. Take some time to reflect on how you can meet the needs you connected with. What can you do to meet these needs before, during and after a presentation or training?

If the need is support, ask a friend for the kind of support you want. Allow yourself to be open to various strategies that could meet your needs.

If it Feels Challenging to Talk to a Group - External Stimuli

This exercise is about how to manage strong emotions about giving a presentation if the stimuli is outside of yourself. It might be something that you hear someone say. Or it may be something that you see someone do, looking away, rolling of the eyes, silence etc.

Anything specific in the exterior circumstances that creates a feeling of nervousness, insecurity or some other strong feeling. Imagine that the worst (or something you are really worried about) happens, and for every thing that you think of, make sure you make it an observation. If needed, take the time to transform any evaluation into a clear observation. Use this exercise either generally, to prepare yourself before you perform a presentation, or prior to meetings with a specific audience or a specific moment that you are extra concerned about.

1. What's the worst that could happen to you when you lead a seminar or talk to a group?

    Some common examples used to be if someone were to fall asleep, to walk out, to say something special, to scream or to cry. Make a note of incidents that could transform a presentation into a challenge. Catch as many as possible and turn them into observations. Make a list.

2. What do you tell yourself that this (point 1) means? What do you say about yourself (labels, ratings)?

3. What do you say/think about the person - the stimuli (point 1) in this situation? (labels, judgments)?

4. Translate what you say about yourself – into the feelings and needs that this is trying to express?

    Take your time to get a deeper connection with these feelings and needs.

5. Translate what you say about the other person into your feelings and needs.

    Take plenty of time to get a deeper connection with these feelings and needs.

6. What do you guess is happening within the other people when they act as they do (1)? Thoughts, feelings, needs and requests.

7. What can you say or do to get a deeper connection to the others in this situation?

How can you express the needs you discovered in points 4-6? Take some time to consider if there are any strategies that would help you to meet these needs. What can you do to meet those needs before, during and after a seminar or training? How can you express your requests?

Expectations and Demands on Yourself

1. Write down the expectations, demands and labels you put on yourself? Are there some things you often say to yourself when you judge something you have done?

   Complete the following sentences:

   - I expected that I would ...

   - By now I should ...

   - I should be more ...

2. What needs are you trying to meet through what you are saying to yourself?
3. What do you feel when connecting to those needs?
4. What can you do to address these needs?

   Make sure it is not strategies that can turn into demands or add to the expectations.

Motivation for Leading Groups

It is useful to know why you want to lead groups, if you really want to act in a way that benefits the group and its goals. The clearer you are about your purpose, the more you can influence and lead in a direction you value and believe will contribute the most.

Many leaders and managers I have coached have said they have been surprised of how often they have felt loneliness or separation in their leadership role. Contrary to what you might think, it might be a challenge to meet your need of belonging or community being the leader of a group. This feeling of loneliness might become a major pitfall if not handled. Many leaders unconsciously end up "buying love" in different situations[2], in an attempt to feel that they are a part of the group. Feelings of loneliness can make it harder to set much-needed limits or to question things in a constructive way because you are so keen to be part of a community.

---

[2]. By the term "buying love" I mean being willing to do things just to get others to like me.

Make sure to nurture your need for community in other ways, if you have a leadership position. If you are not aware, one of your motivations behind being a leader will be companionship and you might struggle to have that met and at the same time lead with integrity.

If you are clear about your intention, it is easier to make more aware choices about how to handle different situations. One way to become more aware of your motivations is to ask yourself how you react when a leadership situation does not turn out in the way you wanted it to? What happens in you at the thought of it? Do you feel worried, scared or annoyed? Do you feel hopelessness or despair?

For example, if you are longing for fellowship, remind yourself that this need seldom will be met in the leadership role. The participants may question what you are doing, make demands, or choose not to participate. Reminding yourself that your need for community can be met in other contexts can help you to relax.

When we are aware of the needs we want to meet by leading a group, it is easier to look out for the pitfalls. Some of the needs that tend to be particularly important to explore as far as leadership is concerned are community, efficiency, creativity, freedom, reciprocity, to contribute, to be seen, love and acceptance.

As a leader it is easy to become so much of a part of a group that you lose perspective, especially if what drives you to take on the leadership of a group is that you value connection. You may be afraid of the feeling of loneliness and want to be friends with everyone in a situation where it does not serve the group. One benefit of being aware of the need for community is that it helps you focus on taking everyone's needs into account.

If your strongest need is to be seen and you are not aware of it, you may fall into the trap of "buying love." It will show up in various ways. One is that you do not devote as much attention to everyone's needs, so if a person seems to see you more than others, he or she might also get more of your attention.

Another way it shows itself is that you come up with solutions before the time to focus on solutions is ripe, you take more space than what is constructive, or that you use the fancy explanations for what happens without it being warranted.

What Needs Do You Want to Meet By Leading Trainings and Seminars

Use the questions below to get clear about what is your driving force and become aware of your pitfalls.

1. Start by finding out which of your needs you want to meet by leading. As a support you can use the list of needs in the end of this book. If you have difficulty in recognizing your intention using only words that describe needs, you can complete the sentences on the next page.

   From there, you will get clues about what needs you want to meet through leading trainings. Allow the thoughts to flow freely, that way you will have the best chance to discover the ideas that will give you important information.

What I dream of when leading the group is ...

Something that really matters to me is ...

If I could choose, people would always ...

When I lead a group, what I dislike the most is ...

The worst that can happen when I stand in front of a group is that ...

One sign that I'm not good enough as a leader is ...

The perfect leader...

   Another way to do this is to remind yourself of how you want to feel after leading trainings. Read what you have written and see if you can find the needs that "cry out for attention" behind these sentences.

2. Think about and write down at least three other ways to meet these needs other than to lead trainings. It helps to connect to your freedom of choice, which makes it easier for you to be clear about what it is you value in leading trainings.

Useful reminders

- Remind yourself that there are always different ways to meet a need. The fact that you feel nervous, unsure or stressed says nothing about your ability to share NVC or any other subject. One thing that has helped me, is to think that we are not afraid of the *reactions* of others, we are afraid that we will not be able to handle those reactions.

- Remind yourself to pay attention to your own reactions, as those are what you can change. Something that really makes nervousness and stress increase is fighting it, not acknowledging it and trying to force those feelings to go away!

- Remind yourself that the response you get from others will depend on how they are hearing you. What you can do is help them to hear you in other ways.

- Remind yourself that it is not your nervousness that will bother others the most. What is often most disturbing is if you try to hide what you are feeling and if they, at the worst, start focusing on taking responsibility for how you are feeling instead of on the content you want to share with them.

Chapter 3

To Plan or Not To Plan, is That The Question?

Checklist - Design and Content

I sometimes hear people say that they avoid planning because they want to be in the present moment and act spontaneously. For me a plan contributes to greater security, which makes it easier for me to be present and to deal with what comes up spontaneously. In order to be able to do so I have to let go of my plan whenever I see that it is not serving me.

When it comes to planning, there is evidently a difference between half-day presentations and longer trainings. When giving NVC trainings of some length, I make a more general plan, knowing that the participants usually make requests that will influence the direction of the content as soon as the class starts.

When I have a plan it is also easier to focus on and to determine what material to prepare and what to bring, for example, handouts, books and other material. When planning, the questions below may be helpful.

1. Is this your only or initial meeting with the group?
Your plans usually depend on whether you will meet with the group only once or for several times.

Not only does the time at your disposal influence the way you teach, it also determines what materials to bring and how to engage the participants in the most efficient way.

2. What do you know about the participants?
Are all the participants members of the same organization, workplace, or association, or not? Your planning will differ if you have reason to believe that the participants already know one another and if they don't.

3. What if the participants belong to the same organization?
Most organizations are hierarchically organized and it may be valuable for you to know whether there are managers, teachers or anyone else in positions of authority among the participants? The presence of people from different levels in the organization and/

or lack of equality between the participants may reduce the willingness to be open and honest. Is there a history of open conflict within the group, or do you have reason to believe that there is an ongoing conflict between some members in the group or between groups within the organization?

4. Do you already know some of the participants?
Knowing some of the participants in advance has certain advantages, but may also put you at risk of connecting more easily to the ones you know, which perhaps sends the wrong signal to the other participants in that they are "not seen or heard."

5. How many people will attend?
It is helpful to know the number of participants, both for material preparation, but also because certain exercises work better in smaller groups and others in larger groups. Sometimes an introduction is "open" and you have no idea who or how many will attend, the size of the room being the limit. In that case, you might want to have a few different loose plans to choose from.

The group

If you are to work with an established group, such a working group, or a team, it may be useful to find out more about the group in advance. For example:

- What do they expect to get from you and your presentation?
- What information have they received about you or your subject before you see them?
- I usually ask to see the invitation - if there was a written one - to get the exact same information as they have received.
- Do they have any special focus in their job, where hearing about some particular part of NVC would be of use?

- Are there explicit values/problems in this group? If that's the case you can start from there when you plan.

- Are there topics that you think are particularly important to touch on in this group? Even ones that they themselves have not thought about?

- Are there some special problems to tackle in this particular group? Any pitfalls to look out for? Or are there some topics that might be taboo or really hard to address?

Prepare and be aware

If you are going to meet an existing group, it might be worthwhile to prepare for various pitfalls. But be aware that your assumptions may be entirely wrong, and stay open to surprises. If you have listened to a description of the group by the person that hired you, remember that it is only this person's perspective that you have received. I've been surprised more than once and therefore a bit out of focus, when I have, for instance, been informed that the group consists of people labeled as "unmanageable," who have turned out instead to be - in my view – "very cooperative."

I have sometimes met groups with open or unvoiced conflicts – within the group, conflicts that the person who engaged me was hoping for me to settle, yet without telling me about it. On one occasion 70 percent of the group was told, just minutes before I arrived, that they were going to lose their job. It took me some time to realize this and the fact that they were not at all open for participating in some exercises, as what they all needed was empathy and clarity.

Conflicts or other challenges that the group is facing may make it unsafe to use exercises that are not fully accepted by all of the participants. You may even find it challenging to be honest. If on the other hand the group is open to handling conflicts, they will have an outstanding opportunity to maximize their learning and the integrating of communication skills. Usually some participants are eager to talk about the conflict, while others may be reluctant – if for example the manager is present.

If you meet a group - with an ongoing conflict - only once, or if you are pressed for time - you usually contribute more if you teach some specific skills rather than try to manage the conflict as such and then leave them with what has come up without having presented to them the tools to continue.[1]

6. Why are the participants coming to your workshop?
Different participants have different motives. Some are interested in how to express something that seems like a challenge or how to manage conflict resolution at work. Others would like to understand more about communication with kids, and some would like to learn how to handle challenges in a group. Other topics of interest could be how to formulate a certain message, how to communicate with a particular person, or how to mediate a conflict.

Their expectations often are related to the information they have received about your training, workshop or seminar. Give people what they are there for, or what you promised before the training, without budging from your values. Or at least communicate about why you cannot deliver what they were promised.

7. Is participation voluntary?
Are some participants attending your workshop because they think they "must" or "should" do so? Has someone promised them some kind of reward if they participate, or punishment if they choose not to do so? The less choice people experience, the more important it will be to recognize and deal with their need for freedom of choice. Before they get in touch with their own free will, it is difficult to learn anything at all.

8. The timetable
Make sure that everyone has the same information about the schedule; when to start, when to break for lunch and/or coffee etc.? Will all participants show up and leave at the same time? If the par-

---

[1]. Read more about Mediation in my book *A Helping Hand. Mediation with Nonviolent Communication*.

ticipants belong to an already established group, it usually is more efficient and energy saving to stick to their normal schedule. Follow the agreed upon schedule as far as possible, otherwise some of the participants may lose focus on your presentation. Read more about this under "Ideas on how to end" and "Finish in time."

Structural issues are more important than you might think as tools to provide trust, connection and safety. The impact of uncertainty around the schedule can vary and depends on the individuals, the group and the culture. Since openness is an important part of NVC, it can be supportive to use some time and energy on creating trust between you as a facilitator and the participants, trust that is the basis for honesty and openness. This holds for all trainings in which you spend time together for more than one day. Of course, the honesty and openness will be practiced on a level that suits the individual group's purpose and goals.

When you are clear about the points above, continue with the following questions:

9. What do you hope for during your time together?

The clearer you are about what you hope the participants will profit by through the training or presentation, the easier it becomes to determine what kind of activities to choose. You may have different aims for what you want them to experience, for example:

Inspiration: This can be done by showing the participants how they can use the steps of NVC in their everyday life by telling stories where it becomes clear what role NVC has played in the life of others.

Skill building: Choose exercises that will allow participants to practice different communication skills.

Connection: If the participants are looking for ways to create a deeper connection between the members of the group, use short exercises or games focusing on sharing experiences.

Exploration of and experiencing differences: Perhaps you want someone to experience the difference between being heard with sympathy and being heard with empathy. In this case you choose exercises or activities that invite the participants to listen to others and to express themselves. You might experiment with different types of role plays or try to transform challenging messages into "ease-to-hear" messages.

Intellectual understanding: You might focus on describing the different steps of NVC, it's basic principles and key differentiations[2] in order to paint a clear and understandable picture of the process.

Having fun: There are many games and easy to practice exercises that can be useful in learning how to communicate with the help of NVC.

10. How to be seated?

The circle is the fundamental geometry of open human communication
    Owen Harrison[3]

Since time immemorial, people have been sitting in a circle to talk, manage conflict and to make decisions. Most people know the myth of King Arthur and the Knights of the Round Table. Arthur fostered cooperation and cultivated unity by building a round table for his knights, all of whom were equal in their deliberations. Research from the UBC Sauder School of Business shows the mythical king ideas made sense. The researchers put experimental groups in circles or squares and discovered that when they were seated in a circle they were more focused on friendship and care for one another, while those in squares became more focused on self success. The circle has no top or bottom, no sides to take. In a circle, we simply meet, face to face. To sit in a circle seems lika a natural way to socialize for many people. One of the researchers, Juliet Zhu, claims

---

2. See the appendix on page 92but also the book *Cracking the Communication Code. Nonviolent Communication by 42 Key differentiations*. Hoffman & Larsson.
3. Owen, Harrison (1999) *Open Space Technology A User's Guide*. Berrett-Koehler Publisers.

that "the geometric form we are sitting in, is subtly affecting us by stimulating our needs for togetherness or individuality."

In most NVC trainings I have participated in or led, we have sat in a circle. I have chosen to use a circle for a few different reasons. First because in a circle everyone can see one another and therefore dialogue is facilitated. The shape also makes it easier for everyone to hear everyone else. The circle therefore facilitates interaction in a way that no other ways to sit do. The values that NVC stands for; the reciprocity and listening to everyone's needs, are supported by this way of sitting. Sitting in a circle has been used around the world for millennium, but can, still feel strange to those who are accustomed to, for example, sitting in rows. The tension is usually eased when people discover that in this way everyone may have a greater impact on what you do together. This is part of the beauty of sitting in a circle, the power is distributed between all and all can easily be heard and seen by everyone else. It also reinforces the connection between the participants when they see each other instead of looking forward at the leader only. In many trainings and conferences where NVC is shared, The Open Space Technology inspires the structure. It is a conference form founded by Harrison Owen and makes it possible for the skills and knowledge of the whole group to have a place.[4]

Don't use a circle because you think you "have to." In some rooms and in some contexts, the circle won't work. In that case do whatever best suits the situation.

11. What do you want participants to bring home?

You can, for instance, focus on creating clarity based on a number of assumptions or key differentiations (see appendix) that NVC is based on. You can present one or two situations to practice on their own after the workshop. Having a clear focus makes it easier for you to choose activities and exercises.

Remind yourself that although there are some things you would like the participants to pick up and continue practicing, the participants are the ones deciding what is most important for them. I also try to not cover everything in the same training or presentation as

---

[4] Owen, Harrison (1999) *Open Space Technology A User's Guide.* Berrett-Koehler Publisers.

I know from own experience that NVC is learnt in steps.

12. What strategies are you going to use?
Look back at what you have found out so far and take some time to answer the questions below. Continue with points 10 – 13 to make things even more clear.
  - How do you want to present your main points?
  - What strategies do you want to you use?
  - What methods or what kinds of activities do you want to use; theory, discussions, exercises in couples, or in small groups, or in the whole group.

13. How do you want to open your presentation?
How do you want to introduce yourself and your intentions for this training, workshop or seminar? What can you say that makes both you and the participants ready to go into the training?

View suggestions under the heading "The First 5-15 Minutes" in Chapter 1.

14. How do you bring the workshop to a close?
Three questions to ask yourself before the closing of a workshop:
"Do I want to know something about what the participants have gotten out of the workshop?"
"Do I want to evaluate the presentation and what do I want to get out of it?"
"What might the participants want to have space to express and hear from others to end in a supportive way?"

I often end a training event with some kind of sharing of gratitude or focus on how things have met our needs. During NVC- trainings, it is easy to focus primarily on how to deal with challenging situations, difficult conversations, and internal and external forces of different natures, and we tend to forget that one of the strengths of NVC is its ability to shed light on things that are worth celebrating. That is one of my reasons to finish with that in our focus. Another reason is that in this way the participants also become aware of how NVC can be used in situations that have worked out in the way we wished. You can find more suggestions on how to finish on "Ending a Group That Has Been a Group During Longer Time" on page 117

15. What to bring?
If you frequently run trainings or make presentations, a hot tip is to make a "packing list" to be used for every occasion. The list can for example include: Pencils, paper, flip chart, scotch tape, scissors, name badges, handouts, feedback forms, and contact information for those interested in learning more.

16. Pitfalls.
Is there something that is particularly challenging in some particular situation? Something that you can prepare yourself for? What preparations - inner as well as outer - can you do to feel more ready to handle challenges.

Therapy or Training

Studying NVC can trigger emotional processes. They can be both interesting and instructive, but also frightening. Emotional processes can enhance learning, but also distract from learning, for both those who are experiencing strong emotions, and for those who are observing the processes of others.

This, of course, depends on the purpose of the training, why everyone is there, the participants' relationships and so on. I experience it as a great support to be clear about my intention behind teaching NVC. If the purpose of my meeting a group is their learning how to communicate in a different way or to handle conflicts, I am careful not to open up for deeper emotional processes. Instead, I focus on other things that I think contributes more to their learning.

This is especially true in already existing groups that do not feel completely safe together or are not used to vulnerable openness. With these I usually use my more "neutral" exercises. These are exercises in which those who want to can use their own examples, but where the exercise includes examples so nobody has to share something that is challenging for them if they do not want to. See examples of such exercises in Chapter 3 under the title, "The Basic Components of NVC" on page 74. My experience is that the basic principles of NVC itself are already enough for many to "ruminate" on. When someone wants to share personal examples I receive it with empathy and care. As much as possible I let the person him or herself be the one who decides how open she or he wants to be about what is going on inside. When I suspect we are entering areas that will take more time than I would wish, I can express that I want to change the focus. It has sometimes resulted in me staying afterwards to talk to the person if needed. When I teach NVC my purpose is first and foremost to share skills that have been invaluable to me. For me education is more about learning new skills than to handle emotional processes. In certain situations, however, these skills can contribute to our being able to handle things at a new depth within us.

Training Content

Here are some ideas about content depending on the time at your disposal. This is of course just a suggestion, so please take it as a source of inspiration when you decide what to offer.

1 to 2 hours presentations of NVC

Suggestion 1:
The purpose of NVC, examples of what NVC has meant to you, information about Marshall Rosenberg, CNVC, the 4 components, the 2 parts, the basic assumptions and some typical NVC-dialogs. Use short exercises on one or a couple of the basic components. Make them short so you can follow up. Information on where to find more information about NVC. End on time with some sort of feedback/evaluation.

Suggestion 2:
The purpose of NVC, examples of what NVC has meant to you, Marshall Rosenberg, CNVC, a certain aspect, some key differentiations or basic assumptions. Some short exercises around some of the basic components where you connect to the key differentiations or central assumptions you have chosen to focus at. Where participants can find more information about NVC. End on time with some sort of feedback/evaluation.

Half-day NVC-training

Suggestion 1:
Introduction to NVC - Marshall Rosenberg, the 4 components, the 2 parts, purpose, core beliefs and sample of dialogs.

Examples of what NVC has meant to you. Exercises to clarify what you are talking about, such as exercises shedding light upon the four components.

Questions. Evaluation. Give information about where participants can find more information about NVC. End on time with some possibility to give you feedback.

Suggestion 2:
The purpose of NVC, examples of what NVC has meant to you, Marshall Rosenberg, some principles, key differentiations or basic assumptions.

Exercises that clarify the focus you have selected. Adjust the topic to the group, for example, by including some variation of the exercise "Communications Cocktail" or "The four chairs."

Give information about where participants can find more information about NVC. End on time with some possibility to give you feedback.

One-Day NVC-training

- Introduction
- Round of names and answering some kind of question maybe:
- What makes you want to learn about NVC?
- Introduction to NVC - Marshall Rosenberg, the 4 components
- the 2 parts, purpose, core beliefs and a taste of a dialog
- Exercise to clarify the components (maybe in small groups)
- Theory on empathy
- Exercises on empathy (small groups) for example, "Empathy Chairs."
- Basic empathy skills.
- Theory around honesty
- Exercise in honesty and dialog - for example, exercise NVC – Dialog or any of the exercises in saying no.
- Something around appreciation and needs met
- Where participants can find more information about NVC.
- Evaluation of the day
- End on time with some sort of feedback/evaluation.

Two-day NVC-training

- Day 1 the same as the "one day training" above
- Day 2 Introduction to set the tone of the day and remind the group of the intention using NVC
- Reflections and thoughts from day 1 (in smaller groups or in pairs)
- Make the difference clear between communication that connects and communication that makes it challenging to connect. Maybe following it up with Request circles.
- Exercise "Misery Café" and/or exercises on managing anger
- Theory and practice in dealing with anger, shame and guilt (Exercises in "Anger management" in smaller groups)
- Theory and practice in either expressing or hearing "No" (exercises in smaller groups) or do the exercises on worldview and labels.
- Practising expressing and receiving appreciation (small groups and whole group). Expressing appreciation of oneself, of others in the group or someone outside the group.
- Closing Round. End on time with some sort of feedback or celebration of your days together.

Exercises to choose from

- The Basic Components of NVC
- Differentiate Between Observations and Interpretations
- Differentiate Between Thoughts and Feelings
- Differentiate Between Needs and The Strategies to have them met
- Differentiate Between Doable Requests and Non Doable Requests
- Request Circles
- Misery Café (Jackal Café)
- Four choices – Four Ways of listening
- Basic Empathy Skills
- Empathy Chairs
- Communication Cocktail
- NVC dialogue
- Exercises In Dealing With a "No"
- Prepare Yourself For The "No" From Someone Else
- Training On How To Say "No" With The Help of NVC
- Managing Your Own Anger
- Step 2 - Expressing Anger
- The effects of labels
- Worldviews - ideas about human beings and life

Exercises

The Basic Components of NVC

Purpose:
- To bring clarity about the four components of NVC.
- To clarify four basic key differentiations in NVC.

Preparation:

Make a list of sentences of your choice covering Observations, Feelings, Needs and Requests (OFNR). You can prepare a flip chart, a handout or a white board in advance to use the time available efficiently.

These exercises can be modified a lot. They will allow for the participants to take part and be active. Allow a few minutes for each part. Keep the momentums so that you have time to cover all the basic components. Don't let them get stuck in long discussions. Let them know beforehand that they will have only a few minutes for each discussion. Make sure you have time at the end for questions, examples and clarifications.

Differentiate Between Observations and Interpretations

1. Discuss the difference between sentences like, "You are always so negative to new ideas, " and

    "During the meeting, I heard you say at least five things about what you disagree with in what someone has done."

    Which of these statements are interpretations and which describes the behavior of someone?

2. Agree on a behavior (observation) that can be interpreted as follows: "You are always so supportive."

3. Agree on a behavior (observation), which can be interpreted as follows:

"Everyone in that group is selfish, they wants to just grab as much as they can for themselves."

Differentiate Between Thoughts and Feelings

Use the list "List of feeling words" on page 236 and find words that describe what someone may feel when they say;
"I feel loved."
"I feel accepted."
"It feels as if you do not care about me."
"It feels like everyone care only about themselves."
"I feel like I belong here."

Differentiate Between Needs and The Strategies to have them met

a. Discuss the difference between the statements;
"I need to have more time by myself."
and
"I need some inner peace."
Which of these sentences describes a strategy to meet a need and which sentence describes a universal need?

b. Use the list on page 237 and find some of the needs that may be met if the following intention is fulfilled;
"We must make sure people don't get burned out."

c. Use the list page 237. Which of your universal needs could be met if you go to your boss and say:
"I want to get rich."

Differentiate Between Doable Requests and Non Doable Requests

1. Discuss the difference between these four requests:

    "I want you to treat me with respect."

    "I want you to look me straight in the eyes when I talk."

    "I want you to listen to me."

    "I want you to wait until I have finished talking before you start talking, are you ok with that?"

    Identify the sentences that express specific, doable actions and those that do not. Which sentences clearly expresses to the other person what we want them to do?

2. What specific, doable request could you express when you need community or belonging?

3. What specific, doable request could you express when you need to be heard?

4. List some frequently used words expressing, or associating with demands, rather than with requests.

Request Circles

This exercise can be used in groups of three to ten participants. It can be carried out in 10 minutes, or can be extended over a period of one hour if people find it enjoyable and meaningful. Allow playfulness in expressing wishes that are not too carefully prepared.

You can learn to change the way you usually ask for everyday favors and instead use specific, doable requests. This is not about being perfect but about learning. When we are connected to others, requests can be expressed in quite a negligent way and still help us to get things done.

Before you start the exercise you can agree to also practice using Observations, Feelings and Needs, or you may only want to practice the Request part of NVC.

How?

Place the participants in a circle. Person A starts and turns clockwise to person B sitting next to him/her and expresses a request. B will then determine if A's question is a clear, doable request or not. B says "Yes", if what A asks for is perceived as a doable request.

Then B continues clockwise to person C and repeats the procedure with a new doable request. If C says "No," it's because C does not perceive what B asked for as a doable request and explains why. If B does not understand or accept C's explanation the group can help. Give the person who expressed the request, as many chances he or she wants to have to reformulate their pledge till it comes out as a request.

Please note! The person who expresses the request does not need to figure out in advance what to request and how to do it according to the NVC criteria below. You will probably have a lot more fun and learn more if you more spontaneously express a request to the person sitting beside you and only afterwards investigate if your request meets the NVC criteria. Play with a mixture of everyday language and "classical" NVC.

You can use the following criteria to determine whether what someone asks for is a Request or not:
- Is it clear what the person is asking for?
- Is it clear whom the person is asking and when?
- Is it possible to act on or answer to the request in the present?
- Is it doable – i.e. is it possible for anyone to do what the person requests.
- Is it voluntary?

Alternative:
If you want to practice expressing requests to a group of people-do as above but turn not only to the person to the right of you, but to the whole group. The group, or the person to your right, teams up to determine if you expressed a request that is clear and doable or not-according to the criteria above.

Misery Café (Jackal Café)

Aim of exercise:
Learning how to pay attention to and handle language and ideas that hamper or obstruct connection.

Purpose:
- To create awareness about language that makes it challenging to create connection.

- To give this kind of language and the ideas behind it space and acceptance, in order to make friends with it, rather than fighting it.

- Having fun and explore alternative ways to communicate.

- Becoming aware of how we can choose either to contribute to "misery," or to create connection.

- Exploring how different kind of emotions affect our emotions and willingness to keep others well-being in mind.

Materials needed to do the exercise?

Write one A4 card for each of the points below:

JUDGEMENT	good/bad/right/wrong
LABELS	I am/you are/they are
BLAME	fault
DESERVE	punishment/reward
NO CHOICE	can't/have to/must
DEMAND	threat

Procedure
1. Place the cards in a circle on the floor.

2. Let the participants place themselves at random by the cards, at least one person per card.

3. Present a topic of the day relevant to everyone without being personal or intimate. It may for example be road maintenance, local area development, job splitting, dog owners responsibilities, the latest Oscars prizes etc.

4. Start a conversation as if you were in a discussion about the topic you have chosen. Each participant uses language mirroring the text on the card where they are standing. A person who stands by the card "Demands – threat" may use words like must/should/ shall and say something like:

   "Unless the dog owners pick up the dog poop they should be paying a fine or they must be banned from owning dogs."

5. Then the next person answers something that is in line with his or her card. For example, the person who stands by the card "Labels - I am/you are/they are" says:

   "Yes they are true egoists, they care only about themselves."

   Remind the participants that they neither have to agree nor disagree with the statements of others. Allow yourself to take part and act as someone who has an opinion very different from you own.

6. The next person, for example by the card "No choice - Cannot/have to/must ... "and the person says:

   "But you cannot think like that! After all there is nothing to do about it."

7. Make sure everyone says one sentence, or preferably two, and if there are several people at each card, invite all of them say something. If someone does not have something to say, they can just say "pass."

8. When you have completed the dialog, ask the participants to tell how it was and if they learned something.

9. If there is a particular statement where they get stuck, let everyone help in translating it into observations, feelings, needs and requests.

Variations Of The Exercise

1a. Ask the participants to reflect on the words/judgments from the cards that they use most frequently themselves. Ask them to move to that card. There may be several individuals at the same patch. (Maybe have them share shortly on that in pairs).

b. Do the same exercise as above.

2a. Ask participants to reflect on the words/judgments from the cards that they very seldom use? Ask them to move to that card. There may be several individuals at the same card.

b Do the same exercise as above.

3. After everyone has had a turn to say what they want to express, let the dialog flow freely.

4. To enhance the learning, take turns in using your skills in NVC in the dialogs. It will slow down the dialogs as the participants think longer about what to say next, therefore help each other and aim at adjusting the pace to further the learning process forward.

Hints!
- To maintain the involvement and commitment to the chosen topic - ask the participants to keep their statements short.

- This exercise offers a chance to play and explore the effects of different opinions. Be careful not to get caught up in differences of opinions and make sure no one gets too opinionated and has to "stand up for or defend" what they have said later.

- If you as facilitator feel confident to handle the situation, select a topic that participants are engaged in and have opinions about, in order to make room for the "elephant in the room" and open up for views we may hold but usually not express in public. Make sure to differentiate between the subject of getting training in NVC and helping the group to speak about a certain topic.

- This exercise offers an opportunity to let go of self-censorship and permits us to express what we normally see as ruthless, cruel, immoral etc. The aim is not to evaluate what is said but to bring our attention to how we think and how we communicate. Inspired by exercises created by Bridget Belgrave and Gina Lawrie.[5]

---
5. Bridget Belgrave and Gina Lawrie have developed an educational tool called The NVC Dance Floors. Learn more at www.NvcDanceFloors.com

Four choices – Four Ways of listening

This exercise clarifies four different choices we have when talking and listening especially to difficult-to-hear messages. It may be used as part of an NVC-introduction, or in advanced trainings depending on the participants' interests and previous knowledge.

Purpose:
- To clarify that we have a choice how to receive someone else's message.

- To practice how to receive a message in a way that supports communication inwards, with ourselves and outwards with the other/others.

- To understand how the way we listen to ourselves is related to how we listen to others.

- To clarify what happens when we hear a message as criticism, threats, or judgments.

- To have fun and explore communication together.

- To give as many participants as possible a chance to practice different ways to receive a message.

Preparations and materials

Place four pillows or chairs in a circle, one for each way to receive a difficult-to-hear message. Use two sets of Giraffe ears and two sets of Jackal ears per group. Place on each pillow/chair an A4 card with the following text or something similar indicating the four different choices one has when hearing a difficult-to-hear message:

- You are wrong" or "it's your fault," or "inwards Jackal." (Jackal Ears turned outwards - hear what is said as if the speaker is criticizing, threatening, judging or moralizing. Respond by blaming the speaker "you are wrong" and add whatever comes up.)

- "It's my fault or" "Jackal in." (Jackal Ears turned inwards – hear what is being said as if something is wrong with me; hear it as criticism, as threats. Respond by blaming yourself.)

- "What do I feel and need?" or "Giraffe in." (Giraffe Ears turned inwards - Listening for what you are observing, feeling, needing and want to request. "What's going on inside me?")

- "Guessing the speakers feelings and needs," or "Giraffe out." (Giraffe Ears turned outwards - Listening for and guessing what the other is observing, feeling, needing and requesting. "What goes on in the other?").

Procedure:
Demonstrate what the four different choices may turn out by asking a volunteer to express something they perceive as a difficult-to-hear message; a short sentence that you ask them to say four times in the same way and with the same tone of voice.
Show how you respond to the message from each of the pillows/chairs.
   Allow for questions, but just enough for the participants to grasp how to start the exercise. It is often easier to "talk about" the exercise instead of doing it. Remind them that confusion often disappears when the exercise has started.

> **Note:** Do not sit on one of the pillows/chairs when you give instructions, unless you are exemplifying what happens on that particular pillow/chair.

How to?

Version 1:
Place one participant on each of the four pillows/chairs and ask them to put on the corresponding ears, i.e. "Jackal ears in," "Jackal ears out," "Giraffe ears in" and "Giraffe ears out." Ask a volunteer to write down a short message that they perceive as "difficult-to-hear" and then ask him or her to read the message to each and one of the participants sitting on the pillows/chairs, in the same way and with the same tone of voice. Begin for example with the person having "Jackal ears out" and ask him or her to respond to the difficult-to-hear message according to the instructions for "Jackal ears out" i.e. by blaming the messenger. If they struggle with figuring out what to answer, help them by giving some examples.

Repeat this with the three remaining positions. Make sure everyone in the group who wants to receive or give a difficult-to-hear message, gets at least one chance to do so.

Many groups find this exercise so enjoyable that they want to explore all sides of it. It can be done many times and in many different ways, time is usually the limit.

Debrief by answering questions and celebrate learning and insights.

Version 2:
Use the same procedure as in version 1, but ask the participants to enter deeply into the dialog through a role play when in one of the "Giraffe choices."

Version 3:
Only one participant is active at the time, practicing all four choices. Someone reads a difficult-to-hear message and the person moves back and forth, from chair to chair, answering in different ways

depending on position. The difficult-to-hear message may be suggested by the person on the chair and read by someone else.

Version 4
If the participants have former experience of NVC they can work in smaller groups supporting each other as in version 3 above.

Version 5
Start the same way as in version 1, but leave the pillows/chairs empty, and ask everyone to write down their answers to the difficult-to-hear message for the four different choices.

Discuss the answers in small groups making sure that all four choices are represented.

Version 6
This version works best in small groups. Place the four chairs in a circle. Invite four participants to take a seat. Start the same way as in version 1:

One participant reading a difficult-to-hear message and one person at the time answering until everyone has answered. Then ask the participants to move one step clockwise and repeat the procedure reading and answering the message. Repeat this – with the same or a new difficult-to-hear message - until everyone has practiced all four choices.

Five hints for those taking active part in this exercise.

- If you are thinking: "This is just too difficult!" – Read the instructions for each of the four choices for example "Jackal ears in," blaming myself. If you move from chair to chair make sure you keep track of where you are sitting. What choice do I have in this chair?

- If you find it difficult to practice "Giraffe ears in" or "Giraffe ears out"; that your answer to the difficult-to-hear message is more like a Jackal-answer, ask for support and try to distinguish between what is actually happening in a situation and what you think about the situation.

- If you're thinking something like:

- "I'll do it my way, I'll say what comes up for me," I guess you need to experience more freedom. Remind yourself that you are always free to choose where to communicate from. To force yourself (or someone else) to communicate from one certain position misses the point and will probably create resistance rather than connection.

- If you start thinking that you can't connect to the person sending the difficult-to-hear message, try the next chair. Sometimes we disconnect or get stuck, in that case it may also be a good idea to try another position, "ears out" to "ears in", for example. The main purpose of NVC is to create connection and this exercise will help you realize that different choices are always there, some of them probably more fortunate than others when it comes to connection.

- If words do not work - ignore them, and just sit there and try to connect through your eyes, mind, body language and let your actions speak!

"If the person you are talking to doesn't appear to be listening, be patient. It may simply be that he has a small piece of fluff in his ear."
Winnie the Pooh

Basic Empathy Skills

The exercise on the next pages is effective in clarifying what we mean by listening to someone with empathy. It is possible for everyone to be involved, even if different people are variously active. Participants can practice the very basics, but also go deeper if there are skills in the group and willingness to try to for example build a role play from the first basic lines.

The exercise can be done in many different varieties and version 5 includes the aspect of how we can address someone with honesty as well as empathy to create a dialogue in which everyone's needs are included.

Version 1:
a. Do the entire exercise on page 85 individually (10-15 minutes).

b. Then share in pairs or in small groups (three to four people) the feelings and needs you have guessed.

c Then take the role of the person making the various statements. Say the sentence and then give each group 2-3 minutes to think about what they might say if they want to respond to what you say in the role with empathy. Remember that what matter is not whether they arrive at the 'right' needs or empathy guess

d. Let some groups try to respond to you with the empathy guess they have decided on.

e. If you have time you can let some of the dialogs continue somewhat longer.

Version 2:
Do the same as in a – c, but let them practice in groups on how these statements can be met.

Version 3:
Do the same as in version 1 or 2, but use sentences that the group wants to work on. Begin the exercise by "brain-storming" together to find various statements you find it challenging to respond to. If it is a large group, you can ask them first to talk in pairs about this. Then write the statements on a flip chart or white board so that everyone can see them. Chose about five different sentences that they can practice on. Divide them into smaller groups and proceed as in version 1.

Version 4:
Do the same as in variations a – e, but select in advance sentences involving
a theme that the group will immerse themselves in.

Version 5:
Do the same as in the a - e. But start by telling that the purpose of the exercise is to establish connection and not just trying to do it with empathy, but also with honesty if they think it works better.

Imagine what A can feel and need in the following example.

1. A says to you: "I just don't want to talk about it."

What do you thing A might feel?	What do you think A might need?

2. A says to you: "Why are you so selfish, do you think only about yourself? "

What do you thing A might feel?	What do you think A might need?

3. A says to you: "First, you ask me to do it and when I have done it you criticize me "

What do you thing A might feel?	What do you think A might need?

4. A says to you: "There was nothing I could do about it, I was completely powerless ... "

What do you thing A might feel?	What do you think A might need?

5. A says to you: "I feel attacked!"

What do you thing A might feel?	What do you think A might need?

Inspired by an exercise I learnt from Miki and Inbal Kashtan.

Empathy Chairs

This is an exercise that fits into groups of from six to about twenty participants. If the group is larger, it is often more helpful to divide it into two circles.

Purpose:
Practice creating connection by responding with empathy. In this exercise I usually focus on how we use language to connect. In a group where all have plenty of experience and earlier training the focus can also be on exploring the intent of NVC.
The exercise also has the potential to alert participants to the importance of self - empathy to hear others with empathy.
It also clarifies in which situations honesty can create more contact than empathy.

Preparations:
Use four chairs or pillows. Place two seats facing each other.
Place a chair behind each of them as in a train compartment. The rest of the chairs are placed in a semicircle. Make sure everyone in the group can hear what is being said.

Instructions to the group:
1. "One chair is for those practicing NVC. Those who sit on the other chair can express themselves in any manner and say what is alive in the moment. The person sitting on the "NVC - chair" is to hear what is said with empathy. In some situations, it does not lead to connecting to meet someone with a empathetic guess and honesty is a better alternative

but remember that we are using this exercise, mainly to practice empathy guesses right now."

When you explain this, it will clarify the exercise if you sit on the chair you demonstrate and give an example of how it may sound at each of the chairs. Do not continue sitting on the chair when you start talking about something else.

2. We will spend two to three minutes on each dialogue. (Or something else if you have decided.)

3. Invite the first round of participants. Ask two people to sit behind the ones at the front, ready to move forward. Explain that this way to sit contributes to simplicity and continuity by there just being a short pause when switching people in chairs.

4. Ask the person on the chair where you are not practicing NVC to say something short (so that there is plenty of time for the second one to practice). Keep it simple, ideally just one sentence. This person expresses what is alive in them or something they want to say. It may be real or imaginary.

The person on the "NVC chair" makes empathy guesses to connect with the feelings and needs of the other person.

5. After one or three empathy guesses (depending on what you have decided on timing and grade of challenge) ask the person who has been practicing to stand up and find the last chair in the circle.

(In the first round the person practicing only take part in one dialogue. In all other rounds, everybody take part in two dialogs and have both roles.)

The person who sat behind the person training, is now moving forward and express something to the person sitting on the chair that has now become "NVC - chair".
At the same time the person sitting behind the person who have moved forward move one step forward to be ready for the next

round.

6. After about 2 minutes (or one to three empathy guesses), ask the person who has sat on the "NVC chair" to stand up and find a new location in the circle. The person behind advances and the activity continues with new empathy guesses. A new person sits down on the empty chair ready for the next round. And then you continue that way.

7. Depending on how much time you have decided to devote to the exercise and the number of persons; continue the exercise until everyone has had a chance to both make and receive empathy guesses at least once. If you have time for more rounds it can be useful to take a pause when everyone has tried both chairs to harvest any learning.

Version:
1. If the group has 8 or fewer persons, the exercise can be repeated or you can choose to have longer dialogs.

2. The exercise can also be used to focus on practicing honesty and to answer with whatever you feel, need and want.

3. For groups that already has some training in NVC it can be a great practice to invite the response to include both empathy and honesty and use a little more time for each dialogue. However, make sure to keep a fast pace so that everyone is given the space to try.

4. The exercise can be done without chairs so that you stand instead of sitting on the floor. Standing can give more momentum in the exercise and be a nice change in a training that contains of a lot of sitting exercises.

Communication Cocktail

Preparation:
Short theoretical exercise on the assumption that the labels, threats and demands can be translated into the needs of the person expressing them.

Materials:
You need small papers for participants to write on. For example divide a A4 paper in four or six parts.

Purpose:
Provide an opportunity to practice dealing with static languages and language that limits our choice.
Provide an opportunity to practice addressing both with empathy and honesty in order to make connection.

Instructions:
Demonstrate this exercise, as it can be quite confusing otherwise. Let them practice in short periods and catch questions in between rather than letting them practice on their own. You can return to this exercise several times and make different versions of it.

Version A:
Use one to three pieces of paper per person. On each note you write a sentence expressing a label, or a judgment that you experience as a challenge to meet. It can be about you or anyone else. It is is something that the person says in a conversation with you. It can be something you have heard or something that you think would be very difficult to hear.

On the Floor

Step 1.
Everyone stand up. The group can either mingle freely, or do the exercise in two circles; an inner circle and an outer circular.
- Select a note and go up to someone in the group. Read one of your statements with the tone of voice that you want the person to get to practice on. The person you face meet what is said with empathy or honesty, what he or she believes creates the most connection at the time.
The dialogue consists of one to three exchanges; do not go deeper than that. When you have read one of your pieces, it is time for the other person to do the same. You work only with a piece of each and then go on to the next person where you are working with the other statement you wrote. Practice on as many people as possible. Use 15 – 40 minutes for this exercise

Step 2
Select one of the statements you have written down and go up to someone in the group. Give the piece of paper to the other person and ask him or her to read it to you. Practice responding to what is said in the way you think creates the most connection; honesty or empathy.
The dialogue consists of one to three exchanges so do not go deeper than that. When you have practiced on one of your pieces, it is time for the other person to do the same. Practice only with one piece of each and then go on to the next where you are working with the one of the other persons statements. Practice with as many people as possible during the time you have decided on.

Version B:
Practice on responding only with empathy guesses to practice your "empathy leg."

Version C:
Practice on responding to what is said by expressing what you feel and the need to exercise your "honesty leg."

Version D:
Practice on responding to what is said either by honest expressions or empathy in order to practice the entire dialogue and to get a flow between expressing and listening.

Version E:
Do the same versions as above (A - C) but practice how to respond to threats and demands. Ask the participants to write threat or a demand on their pieces of paper.

Version F:
Do the same versions as above (A - D) but use them to practice self-empathy. What the participants now write on the pieces of paper are things they say to themselves or about themselves which they find challenging to handle.

Conclude By Asking:
- What did you learn from this?
- Were there any specific statements that you experienced as extra challenging that you want us to practice together.
Is there are statements the participants had difficulties in creating connection with, you can practice them together. Some of the dialogs can also be a beginning of a longer role - play.

Tips!
Make yourself available as support during the exercise. Jump in when needed but do not take over but let them practice.
Ask them to make it more simply if they get stuck all the time.
Ask them to help each other by making the role more connected to what they are feeling and needing.

NVC dialogue

Purpose:
To get practice in creating a dialogue that includes both responding to others with empathy and to express their own feelings and needs.
To get practice in how to assess when empathy or honesty work the best.

Grouping:
Three people in each group. One will act as a coach in the dialogs. Rotate the roles.

Time:
30 - 45 minutes. Depending on how much time you have, you can for example distribute the time of 10 + 5 minutes x 3. You use 10 minutes per person to dialogue and five minutes after each dialogue to talk about what you have learned. Keep track of time in groups so that everyone gets equal time for their dialogue.

Materials:
Make sure you have access to lists of feelings and needs, and remind each other that you can use these as support in the dialogs.

Proposed Instructions and Hints To The Participants:

1. In this exercise you will work with two other people.

2. When you sit in your group, think of someone you have had difficulties in communicating with. Think about what you would say to this person or what he or she tells you that you find challenging to hear.

3. Choose one of the two persons that you want as your partner in the dialogue.

Both use NVC. The third person of the team is the coach.

Tell your partner in the dialogue who he or she is playing the role of, and describe with no more than two sentences what is the difficulty or challenge.

You will have a total of 9 minutes for each person's situation.

4. Start by either expressing yourself to that person by using observations, feelings, needs and requests, or by to asking the other person to say something to you that you have previously experienced as a challenge to connect with.

5. Use your knowledge of NVC and feel free to use the lists of feelings and needs if this is a support for you.

6. If you are the partner in the dialogue, you too use NVC. By that is meant to express your feelings and needs and respond with empathy. Allow yourself to really empathize with what the other person express so that you can experience the shifts that occur in the conversation.

Note!
Here I would like to mention that some respond with, "but he/she would not say anything like that." Remind them that this is an exercise in communicating in a manner that you do not otherwise do to explore the difference it might makes.

7. If you have the role as "coach", focus your attention on whether what the two parties say or do creates connection. If you do not think that what they do contributes to connection, ask indicative issues such as: "Do you want to express again how it is for you?" "What needs do you guess this person has? "What do you feel right now?" Help those involved in the dialogue to remain in dialogue rather than to start "talking about".

8. Repeat the exercise three times so that each one in the group has taken all three roles.

Ideas for Deepening

Option 1:
Ask for volunteers that want to replay their dialogue and maybe go a bit deeper.

Option 2:
Ask participants if they experienced any specific statement as a challenge and then help them in how they can meet it with empathy or honesty or both.

Option 3:
Ask the other person to let go of his or her focus on using NVC and let the expression come in any way it wants.
Encourage the first person to continue to practice NVC, whatever is being said. You may remind the person about both expressing him or her with honesty and to respond to the other with empathy. The coach is now focusing primarily on the person who uses NVC by supporting her or him to express him or herself with vulnerable honesty and to hear the other with empathy.

Pitfalls:

1. Some people find this exercise as such a big challenge that they might want to withdraw from it or to criticize the exercise. Check it's more important to provide them with support, empathy, or more information or to avoid it and do some other exercise.

2. Some may find it difficult and "unnatural" to keep to strict NVC in the conversation. You can use this opportunity to:

a. Provide empathy for people's feelings of anxiety and need for communication that works for them and create connection.

b. Emphasize the difference between "natural" and "habitual" communication.

c. Remind people that we are not proposing they should use just these sentences in real life if they are not comfortable with them - we focus primarily on changing attitudes. Suggest that they practice a while to learn.

d. To meet the participants' need of confidence that NVC can be used in their daily lives, you can talk about that during a training we encourage people to use the model, but after the training it is of course about finding ways to adapt it to different contexts.

Exercises in Dealing With a "No"

My experience is that practice in dealing with no, whether it's to express their own "no" or manage the "no" of others, will help to clarify many of the fundamental principles and assumptions of NVC. It can give clarity about choice, cooperation etc.

When I see what the group struggle with in these exercises, I as a trainer get feedback on what theoretical parts I might need to be clearer about and what the participants need to practice more on. This might be things like being able to differentiate between observations and judgments and requests versus demands. This means that these exercises are excellent to use in training whatever parts of NVC you want to practice.

Before I do the exercises in dealing with "no", I often remind the participants of the below three things. During the practice, I can then remind them of this to help them discover how they could communicate in order to support connection and mutual respect.

- A "No" can be seen as a "yes" to something else. Make sure you get what the is.
- A "No" can be an invitation to further dialogue.
- A "No" can be seen as a signal that we need to listen more and/or express ourselves more clearly.

Example:
If someone says no to my request to talk about something, maybe he or she says yes to his need for rest or respect or some other need. When we get in touch with what this person needs and listen to them with empathy, it opens the door to further dialogue. In that dialogue we are looking for ways to have both of our needs met.

Suggested Approach:
- Ask each participant to go through some of the exercises individually in 10 - 15 minutes. I do this because I see that some people learn a lot by preparing themselves by reflecting on situations of their own. Eventually you can ask those who want to sit alone to do so and invite the others to share in pairs.
- Thereafter the participants can share what they come up to in groups of three to four people. Ask them also to help each other where they have difficulties in finding needs and requests. Let each person get around 10 minutes to start a dialogue and role play with those they "say no" to.

Saying no can be more charged than you think, so encourage participants to take it easy when they support each other to find new ways to cope with the dialogue.

Prepare Yourself for the "No" From Someone Else

1. Think of someone whose "no" you find it difficult to handle. Who is the person?

   Briefly describe a situation where you ask for something she or he says "no" to.

2. What do you feel and need right now when you think about this "No"? (Self-Empathy)

3. Think of the person who says "no." What do you think his or her needs are? Which needs are you guessing that the person says 'yes' to, needs that she or he would like to have met? (Empathy)

Deepening
You can continue to either writing a dialogue, role play or sharing what you have discovered and learned in small groups.

Practice on How to Say "No" With the Help of NVC

The basic idea;
- Get in touch with the needs the other person expresses by his or her request - something you want to say no to but find challenging.
- Connect with which of your own needs that prevent you from saying yes to the request.
- Find a strategy that can meet both yours and the other person's needs.

   1. Think of someone you have difficulties in saying no to. It can be a friend, a child, your boss or someone else. Write down what they ask you about.

   2. Which of their needs are expressed by their requests? (Empathy)

   3. What needs do you say yes to, are you trying to meet – by saying no in this particular situation? (Self-Empathy)

   4. What could you ask that could contribute to both persons needs being met?

   5. What strategy could contribute to meeting the needs of both persons?

   6. What can you say to the other person if you use NVC? Express your observations, feelings, needs and requests.

Deepening:
Practice to proceed with any of the dialogs either by role playing or in writing.

Transform Your Anger

The process of dealing with anger using NVC is not just a verbal process where judgments are translated. It can also deeply affect the person who translates their judgments to needs. Especially in the beginning, time and care is needed to really get in touch with the needs behind the anger and to allow the anger to transform into a more life-serving feeling. Stay with this part of the process until that happens, rather than going further to keep up with more exercises.

Managing Your Own Anger

Step 1:
A. Divide into small groups. Answer the first two questions individually during a few minutes. Once you have done it, help each other in translating all the interpretations to observations. If you already have formulated clear observations in question 2, go to B.

B. Go through the individual question 3 - 5. Then help each other in groups in finding the judging thought and the need.
This is a "critical" point where care and a lot of empathy is needed. For the feeling of anger naturally to shift to more vulnerable feelings behind the anger the person needs to feel secure.
If you have more time, you can also do Step 2 in the exercise.

Step 2:
C. Use about 10 minutes individually to write down answers to 1 - 3. Then role play in small groups and base it on what you have written.

When strong emotions are involved role playing games can take a long time. If you have the intention to do more examples and role plays it's relaxing for those who takes a role if someone else is keeping track of time.
For inspiration about role playing, see chapter 6.

Step 1 - Preparatory

1. Consider a situation where you are angry about something another person has done or does. Describe the situation briefly.

2. Look at what you wrote and then translate all the possible judgments and interpretations to observation-based language that describes what the other person did or said. (Identify what stimulated her anger.)

3. What do you say to yourself is the cause of your anger? (What are the judgments and thoughts you have which are the cause of anger.)

4. What needs are not met in relation to this situation? (Connect with the core of anger.)

5. When you pay attention to these needs, what do you feel? (Pay attention to the many different emotional nuances that exist in anger.)

What Could Have Been Going On Within The Other Person?

6. Guess what feelings and needs of the other person had when she or he was acting in the situation above (2). Write down your guesses.

   (Respond with empathy.)

7. Focus your attention on yours and the other's needs. Be attentive to what you feel when you do that. Are you still angry, or do you feel any other emotions?

Step 2 - Expressing Anger

1. Write down what you might say to the other person by to expressing your observations, feelings, needs and requests.

2. Write down what that person could possibly answer.

3. What feelings and needs are expressed by this person through what he or she say and do? Write down a guess you could express if you want to treat the person with empathy

Once you have done this you can create role plays based on the dialogue in the situations you have written about. Continue in dealing with the others with empathy as well as by expressing your own feelings, needs and requests.

The Effects of Labels

This exercise is s primarily an exercise in becoming aware of how labels and static images control us whether we are the ones using them or when others label us. The exercise provides a valuable experience of "self-fulfilling prophecies" but is not an exercise in how to grow NVC skills.

Follow it up by talking, in pairs or small groups about what you discovered and how you can use the experience in "everyday life". It is a fun and lively introduction to exercises that involves translating labels and static language to feelings and needs.

Time required:
Approximately 15 minutes for the "game part". Talking in pairs 10-15 min. Depending on group size and focus, the follow-up discussion will last for anything from 10 to 30 minutes. So make sure to have at least 1 hour. Make sure to follow it up in the best

possible way for the group you are working with – preferably doing skill-building exercises like "Communication cocktail" or Request circles.

Group size:
The optimal size of the group for the game part is 5 to 8 people. In a large group, divide into smaller groups.

Material:
For each participant you need an adhesive strip big enough to write a label on. The strips are to be put on someone's forehead and stay there for about ten minutes. Prepare the strips before the meeting begins and keep them in a place so that no one can see them.
Examples of labels you can use:

Dominant, clumsy, moralistic, judgmental, inferior, lazy, kind, generous, arrogant, mean, stupid, clever, coward, brave, trustworthy, unreliable, dissident, creative, anxious, provocative, starry-eyed. Mix labels of different kind i.e. those people usually like to hear and those people don't like to hear.

IMPORTANT!
This exercise needs a facilitator i.e. someone who refrains from participating in the exercise. The facilitator writes labels of his or her choice on the strips and puts one on each participants forehead without showing the "label receiver" what label they carry. The facilitator reads the instructions, facilitates the exercise as well as the debriefing afterwards also reminding the participants not to continue using the labels.

WARNING!
Although this is a very playful exercise there is, if it's not used with care, a risk that it will be experienced as unpleasant by some. Therefore it's VERY important that when the facilitator says "stop" or "time out", everyone immediately stops communicating in accordance with the label someone else carries. Remind them that this exercise is just for getting a common experience to reflect on.

Instruction:
Start by reading the instructions out loud, step by step. You can of course use a case of your own choice instead of the one below:

Image that you are a working team planning for a joint celebration. For your first meeting you have about 10 minutes. Everyone in the group will receive a sticker on his forehead. None of you will be able to read the text on your own sticker. Please note that you will learn more from this exercise if you have not seen or even tried to figure out what label is on your own strip.

I will randomly place one of the label-strips that I have prepared in advance on the forehead of each of you. Wait until everyone has got a label before proceeding with the next step. Use the next 10 minutes to communicate with the others as if the label they carry is a true description of them.

This exercise will be more rewarding if your focus is on communicating with others according to the label they have got instead of trying to figure out what label you have on your forhead. Allow yourselves to play, and stretch your creativity in order to be over-explicit in your communication without mentioning the labels. To "be polite" or avoiding talking to someone is a support if it is in line with their label.

It is important that you stop the exercise after ten minutes sharp as some people may find it really challenging or even painful to be treated in a way they are not familiar with, even if they know it's a game. (If you as facilitator think that the exercise is disturbing or painful for someone, you can choose to stop earlier or take a time out.)

Debrief:
If there are many participants and therefore more than one group, allow each group 10-15 minutes to reflect on what they have learned. Ask each and everyone in the group how they were affected by the exercise. Some people may want to remove their label-strip before talking, others are perfectly ok talking about their experiences without knowing, just guessing, what label they carried. Guessing can strengthen the realization of how much power there is in the

labels we give ourselves and others. As always, point out that it's voluntary to tell others about the impact of the exercise.

Debrief questions for the participants:
1. Did you have the impression that you acted in accordance with the label you were given?
2. Did you have the impression that you acted contrary to the label you were given?
3. What was it like for you to take action against others based on the label they had received? Is there something you will think about in this group or in other situations in the future?
4. What did you learn about static language and labels?
5. What did you learn about self-fulfilling prophecies?
6. Is there something you want to say or hear from someone in this group?

Maybe you would like to conclude this exercise by sharing in pairs to be sure that everyone gets a chance to sort out the impressions of the exercise.

One step deeper:
Continue practicing "Worldviews - ideas about human beings and life" on the next page to deepen your understanding of how to overcome self-fulfilling prophecies and static thinking.

Worldviews - ideas about human beings and life

Ideas we have about human beings can be seen as expressions of feelings and needs. To get in touch with feelings and needs behind beliefs/ideas others have, ideas that we disagree with, can help us to "see them as human beings". Whether we share their beliefs or not, we can get in touch with their needs as needs are universal and we have the same needs as the person whose ideas we disagree with.

Our strong reactions to ideas others have may in the same way be regarded as expressions of our feelings and needs.

To learn how to identify and connect with feelings and needs can help us understand ourselves as well as others holding other opinions than ours. Instead of judging and using labels, we can focus on understanding what needs we are trying to meet through feeding the perceptions and opinions we do.

Exercise in five steps

1. Participants work in small groups. Use five minutes to individually write down statements/labels that you have heard others use talking about human beings or life in general. Choose statements/labels that you find difficult to enjoy. Feel free to include labels like:

    "Typical managers to ..." or "(A) always tries to be so ..."

2. Use 5-10 minutes to individually write down any guesses you have on feelings and needs in the person who used the statement/label you have written down. If you can't guess what the feelings and needs might have been, ask your fellow group members if they have a suggestion.

3. Use 5-10 minutes to write down feelings and needs present in you when you heard the statements/labels you have written down.

4. As a follow-up, share with your group what you have noted

in 1-3 above, and support each other with finding feelings and needs behind statements/labels where you are in doubt or when you are having difficulties.

5. Use any of the statements you wrote down in a role play.

The role play includes two roles. One participant (A) has the intention to connect using NVC when another participant (B) is expressing his/her "point of view". B uses "not too difficult to hear" statements/labels in order to optimize the chances for people to learn from the role play. You can start using written down statements and then improvise. Role player "A" tries to either guess "B's" feelings and needs or express his/her own. The rest of the group takes part as observers, and if requested as supporters.

If you don't have previous experience of simulations or role playing it may be of help to read the section "Role playing - some ideas of how to do it" on page 151.

Suggested structure:
Write down at least six statements/labels and guesses on yours as well as the other person's feelings and needs. Use the following structure.

a. Statement: _____

b. What might the person who says this feel and need?
_____

c. When I hear this statement/label I feel _____ because I need _____

Example: How to hear a statement using NVC:

a. Statement:
People are just trying to grab as much as possible for themselves.

b. What might the person who says this feel and need:
Maybe the person who says it feels anxious and irritated because he/she needs reassurance that resources are shared mutually and with greater care than it's done.

c. When I hear this statement/label:
When I hear you say "People are just trying to grab as much as possible for themselves" I feel frustrated and annoyed, because I need to trust that we all wish each other well and want to contribute to the enrichment of life. How is this for you to hear?

Evaluate = Harvest Learning

When you're in the middle of a presentation or class, it is difficult to evaluate how the activity has met yours and the participants needs. I suggest you end each presentation or training by some kind of evaluation. If you ask for observations, feelings and needs, you can get invaluable information and at the same time it is a practice for the participants to formulate responses in these terms.

Some things I usually ask for:
- To be told which activities, meetings or other (observations) that met their needs.

- To hear what we have done, or have not done that have not met needs. This is for me significantly more useful than to being told if someone thinks what I have done was good or bad.

- Feedback that may make it easier for me to see what needs I contributed to meet and what I can change to help in meeting other needs.

What I do not want to encourage include:
- Feedback that feeds the habit others and I have to think in comparison, or blaming ourselves.

- Feedback that would make me "brag" me and think I am better than others.

On next page there is an example of a structure that can be used for evaluation.

Evaluation

Your name (optional): _____

1) On a scale of 1-6, identify how well your needs were met. Leave blank if you cannot relate this need to this training.

Need	Not met			Very much met		
Learning	1	2	3	4	5	6
Useful knowledge	1	2	3	4	5	6
Clarity	1	2	3	4	5	6
Inspiration / hope	1	2	3	4	5	6
Self-Understanding	1	2	3	4	5	6
Understanding of others	1	2	3	4	5	6
Other_____	1	2	3	4	5	6

2) Did the trainer contribute to your needs being met?

Contributed by no means			Contributed a lot		
1	2	3	4	5	6

3) How did contribute to getting your needs met?

Contributed by no means			Contributed a lot		
1	2	3	4	5	6

4) How satisfied are you with the training?

Contributed by no means			Contributed a lot		
1	2	3	4	5	6

Tell us about your feelings, needs and observations in relation to the training as a whole.

5) Do you have any suggestions about changes in the structure or content?

6) Anything else?

How Was It?

In addition to asking the participants for feedback, you can get a lot out of taking the time to a personal evaluation of what you have done. Make sure that also your own evaluation of your effort is based on the needs being met and needs not being met.

If you want to learn the maximum, pay attention to what you judge to as good or bad long enough to understand which need you wanted to take care for in that way and then connect with the needs. Perhaps you are happy with some part of the presentation or training and displeased with another. Let both have a place.

If you think a presentation or training was a failure, it is important to find a way to manage your disappointment because otherwise it can easily grow. When you can approach disappointment, curious to see what is the core of it, you can learn a lot.

When I think that I have failed, it may be difficult to find motivation to try again, fearing that the same thing might be repeated. Therefore it is important to have effective ways to "mourn" what has happened, learn from it and find the power to try again.

The first step to morn - in such a way that you can learn from your mistake - is to get in touch with which of your needs were not met by something you did (or did not do). Take a moment to deepen the connection with these needs. This can clarify what you value and how you can move on. The second step is to get in touch with the needs you were trying to meet with what you did. When they are clear to you, consider whether you can think of other ways to meet those needs while leading. The ability to quickly translate your inner critical thinking, both about yourself and others, are invaluable for a teacher. This you can practice each day.

Please use the questions on the next page as aid if they help you getting inward connection. Remember, you can also use others as support.

Evaluating Your Effort as the Trainer

Use this evaluation after you have led a training to learn more about how you can meet both your own and others' needs more effectively during a training or presentation.

1. Start with writing down what you say to yourself. Give free space to your thoughts. The more you allow yourself to be honest with what you're thinking, the more you get out of the exercise. Do you make any judgments of yourself and your skills? Are there any internal demands; some "shoulds" or "musts" you think you have not lived up to? Do you put any labels on yourself?

2. In what situation did these thoughts turn up? Look for clear observations on what you did that you are particularly satisfied or dissatisfied with. What was it you did that you reacted on and that you would have liked to do differently?

3. What do you feel when you think of this? Stop for a moment and really allow those emotions to take place.

4. What needs are these feelings telling about? That is, which of your needs were met and what did not happen the way you were acting?

5. Focus for a moment on the needs that were met, and enjoy the possibility you have to enrich your own and others' lives.

6. Take a moment to really let all your answers sink in and think about what you can learn from this next time you want to hold a presentation or training?

    Can you imagine how you could now be able to meet the needs you came to in paragraph 4?

Is there something you can use as reminders for the next time you are giving a presentation or training?

Ending a Group That Has Been a Group During Longer Time

The closure of a group will affect what the participants bring with them because it is their last impression from group.

I usually consult the group and also to ask myself if there is something special that needs to be addressed in order to finish.

Evaluation can be done in lots of ways so use your creativity to create what suits this group. For some it fits to express how it has been for them in writing, others want to express it verbally, someone might want to express themselves with images and symbols, so I usually try to offer alternative ways. Many times, an evaluation provides the participants the opportunity to express both disappointments and gratitude, and can function as a kind of ceremony that makes it easier to end.

A study group, in contrast to such groups as a work group, often stops at a predetermined time, which also affect what is taking place in the group. People may be prepared to take greater risks in a group that they know will end. Some can also be less motivated to influence a group of the same reason. The longer a group has existed, the more importance, I give to the ending.

Part 2

Leading the group

Chapter 4

Dilemmas + Challenges = Nutrition for Growth

Dilemmas That Can Help You Grow

Here are some of the dilemmas that many who have given trainings and seminars have encountered and some suggestions on how you can manage them by using NVC. Being willing to face these challenges may indeed help you learn and grow.

Some key differentiations are selected for each dilemma as extra support to gain clarity around each dilemma. Read more about key differentiations in the appendix on page 225.

The Key Differentiations help us to explain a not so well known - or even unknown – concept, through a more familiar one. It is a lot easier to describe a tandem bicycle if we can start by describing how it differs from a regular bike, assuming a bike is an object the other person is familiar with. If we want to say something about the Japanese instrument koto, it is easier if we can start with a harp, dulcimer, or a Swedish keyed fiddle. We do not in this case claim to have categorized all stringed instruments as kotos, kanteles or keyed fiddles. We describe the differences between them but we do not say anything about their quality. We do not imply that one is "right" and the other "wrong" or that one is better than the other. We just want to answer the question: "What's the difference?" Just the fact that the question is asked is as important as how someone answers it as the question makes people reflect.

When You Do Not Get a Response

Dealing with this dilemma, it helps if you are clear about the difference between "demands and requests" (key differentiation 11) and to "Persisting vs. demanding "(key differentiation 18).

Sometimes it is difficult if a group is silent when you would like to have a response. You can then express any request to the group that will make it easier for people to participate at the level they are comfortable with. Their motivation to respond might increase if you express your own feelings and the needs that you hope that their answers will meet.

When they see that you are human and that they can help you, they will be more willing to say something. You could, for example say:

I need more connection and I get a little bit nervous when I do not hear any answers to my questions. Does anyone want to express something about why you have been silent so far?

Or,

I notice that I am a bit puzzled when I hear no response to my questions. I would like to have more clarity around whether what I have been talking about so far has been of interest to you. Does anyone want to express how you think you might benefit from what I am talking about?

If everyone still remains silent, then there are several ways to continue. I could, for instance, assume that they do not feel safe talking in this group, so then I try another strategy to find the connection I need with the group. For example, I could try this:

I would like to see a hand up from all those who do not feel safe at the thought of being the one who first says something?

Or,

I would like to see a hand up for all who experience what I have been talking about as interesting and want to hear more about it.

On one occasion I held a training and felt sure that the evaluation at the end would reflect a lack of interest. During the day long training most of the group was silent, except when I put them to work in small groups to do some exercises. I had tried all kind of "tricks" to connect but it seemed like I was getting nowhere. In the end I realized I could ask them to tell me more about how it was for them to talk in the large group or to give examples when I asked for it. I added these questions to the ones I usually ask to get an evaluation about if the training had worked for them or not.

To my amazement, the evaluations of the training were overwhelmingly positive. Some stated that they felt overwhelmed and that they did not say much because they had wanted time to digest the information because it seemed so valuable to them. Some mentioned that they were thinking of making changes in their lives and that was one of the reasons behind their seemingly not being active.

What I had assessed as skepticism, boredom or disinterest was simply that they needed more time to reflect. I was of course astounded and at the same time happy that I had asked them to write an evaluation - as I would have otherwise believed my own assessment to be true.

See more about evaluating under the heading "Evaluate = Harvest Learning" on page 112.

When someone is Talking Longer Than You (or the group) Want to Listen

To deal with this dilemma, it helps if you are clear about the difference between "Emphatic sensing versus intellectual guessing" (key differentiation 25) and "Protective versus punitive use of force" (key differentiation 4).

As a workshop leader or a trainer, it is useful to be able to interrupt when someone is talking longer than what serves the group, you or the person themselves. When you stop someone in a group where you wish to maintain connection and to make sure that everyone's needs are heard, you have a chance to demonstrate either the concept of empathy or honesty. You can do so by responding to the person you want to interrupt with a guess of what needs the person wants to meet by talking about what he or she is talking about. You can also interrupt by honestly expressing what you feel or need, and end by expressing a request that can be implemented.

If you as a leader forget to end with a request, it may make it difficult for the person you are interrupting to hear what you are saying as anything but criticism or a demand. When I interrupt with an empathic guess it may sound something like this:

I guess that what you're talking about is really important to you and you really want us to understand the importance of freedom of choice (or some other needs)?

Or with honesty:

I find that I am a bit restless and anxious. Restless because I do not know how long your history will take and I want to make sure that we have time for X. How would it be for you if we proceed with X now?

Many times it is efficient to use both empathy and honesty:

I guess that what you're talking about is really important for you. I want your needs to be met and at the same time I am worried that if you continue it will take more time than I would want us to spend on this, as I also want the whole group to have a chance to have their needs met. I wonder if you are willing to take a deep breath, consider what more you want say and if you want something back from on of us?

Interrupting often creates - contrary to what one might think - more security and trust in you as a leader. Often interrupting is equated with being rude. When I interrupt with NVC, I do it with the intention to create more connection, not to make someone shut up. The purpose is to help meet as many needs as possible, even the needs of the speaker.

When you interrupt because something does not meet your need to contribute to the group, while respecting the person talking, you indicate that you want to preserve certain values and want to help the group to reach its goals.

Another situation where it is worthwhile to interrupt is when a conflict occurs between team members and you want to act as a third party. To avoid escalation of the conflict, you can interrupt anyone starting to use nicknames or labels, or using threats or demands.[1]

---

1. In my book on mediation – *A Helping Hand, Mediation with Nonviolent Communication*, there is

When Someone is In Strong Need of Empathy

To deal with this dilemma, it helps if you are clear about the difference between "Emphatic sensing versus intellectual guessing" (key differentiation 25) and "interdependence versus dependence or independence"(key differentiation 15).

I sometimes use the metaphor that NVC is based on two legs. One I call the empathy leg, which is all about listening, the second I call the honesty leg, which is about expressing ourselves honestly and openly. Communication can be seen as a dance and it will be easier to dance when we use both legs. Listening with empathy for the feelings and needs of another, and also expressing our own, will help us to move forward in the communication.

When a leader uses "the honesty leg" during a presentation or in a class, they are expressing how something we see or hear affects us. If we want to protect connection, it is essential to finish what we say with a specific request. It gives everyone clarity about what we want them to do with the information they have just received from us. This can be particularly valuable during a presentation, as it will both contribute to safety and connection and because it shows how the process of NVC can help a dialog forward. Switch between the two legs, so that the communication becomes a dance.

Do not over-use one of the legs. For example, it might be tempting to stand a long time on the empathy leg if we know the tremendous effect on connection empathy can have. When we learned NVC it might have been the first time we experienced ourselves being heard in depth and we want to give that beautiful experience to others. However, Nonviolent Communication is based on both self-expression and listening to others and that it may contribute to insecurity if you never express what is going on inside of you. Some people may hesitate to express their feelings and needs openly as it may seem too threatening. This applies both to groups in which participants have known each other before, or when they have not.

---

a chapter on interrupting.

If your attempt to listen to students with empathy allows them to express more of themselves than they are completely comfortable with, it may in the long run create less safety in the group.

Sometimes it is very difficult to determine, but it is useful to be aware that openness can at times be experienced as threatening. Therefore keep your attention on someone just as long as that person seems to be okay with it. In a group where NVC is new, I rarely do more than one or two "empathy guesses" to one person at a time, if the person does not express a wish to be heard.

The situation might change if the participants have known each other from before or have had ongoing conflicts in the group, and this is the reason behind their being there; if they have really wanted to attend the training or not, or are listening to you during a presentation at their workplace because the manager has asked them to attend.

In different situations, talking about feelings is accepted differently. Things such as using terms like "Do you feel...?" or " I feel..." are experienced in some groups as very threatening. If I notice this, I can focus my empathy guesses on presenting only observations, needs and requests and skip the feelings part.

In many groups it may contribute to increased acceptance of feelings if somebody has cried or expressed anger. Something else that opens up greater acceptance around emotions is to have a dialog about how unspoken – but felt - emotions affect others. Be careful to notice if someone is trying to send hidden messages to anyone else in the group. You can encourage openness about this by asking questions such as, "Now we've talked about this for a while and I wonder if parts of what we have been talking about exists in this group?"

When You Get Challenging Questions

To deal with this dilemma, it helps if you are clear about the difference between "Self-Empathy versus acting out, repressing, or wallowing in feelings"(key differentiation 23) and" Power with versus power over" (key differentiation 5).

There are some issues and questions that are repeated when you introduce NVC to a group or have a lesson on the subject. These questions can contribute to more clarity if you can answer them in a way that is in line with the principles of NVC. Many of us shudder over certain questions and think that they are difficult to answer or are not sure we have any answers that we are fully committed to.

How you respond to a question will affect your connection with the group just as much as your answers. Sometimes, people's requests to get certain information may be an unconscious request for support to meet their needs of empathy. In many cases, it is therefore constructive to respond to people with empathy or at least a reflection of what you have heard before giving information. In preparation for the presentation of NVC, you can try answering the following range of questions.

Pay particular attention to whether there are any questions you are afraid that people will ask. It might, of course, be a different set of questions you feel uncertain about and want to prepare by getting practice with them. Prepare how you can respond to each of the following questions with an empathic guess of what the inquirer feels and needs, and also how you can give them the information that answers the question.

1. Won't you be treated like a doormat if you talk like that?
2. What is the difference between empathy and sympathy?
3. How can we make sure that everyone's needs are considered?
4. What happens when people do not act in a rational manner?
5. Does this really work in a workplace or with officials?
6. Isn't NVC a cult?
7. How can you determine who will speak next, if you don't have any rules?
8. Will it really make any difference if I listen to someone with

empathy?

9. Do you really think that all people are good?

10. How can I communicate with those who do not use NVC?

11. Whats all this bullshit about needs?

12. Do you really believe that there is nothing we have to do?

13. But isnt it all about being honest and saying no?

Examples:
To address the first question in the manner I suggest, you may say something like this;

Is it so that you are concerned that to talk as I suggest will not give you or us the respect we need? Would you like to hear my view on it?

And if the answer is yes, I may continue:

My experience is quite the opposite, I feel that people are quite respectful when I am clear about what I need and want, do you want to hear an example?

Or,

I'm not quite sure what it is I might have said that has given you that impression, could you say what it is that you fear will be the outcome?

When you hear challenging messages

To deal with this dilemma, it helps if you are clear about the difference between "Self-Empathy versus acting out, repressing, or wallowing in feelings" (key differentiation 23) and" power with versus power over (key differentiation 5).

There is no such thing as a problem without a gift for you in its hands. You seek problems because you need their gifts.[2]
Richard Bach

It may not be these questions that you are most worried about,

2. Bach, Richard (1977) *Illusions: The Adventures of a Reluctant Messiah*

but rather how to handle statements or opinions. Strong opinions can, just as questions, be a great opportunity to both demonstrate how to use the process when we have different views and to clarify the principles of NVC.

Try to answer the following statements and make use of both empathy and honesty to create connection. Prepare how you can respond to each of the statements. Practice responding in a way that includes an empathic guess of what the inquirer feels and needs as well expressing yourself. Put relationship and connection first.

1. This is an unnatural and mechanical way of talking.
2. You just cannot trust some people.
3. This is just another way to manipulate.
4. You cannot use this on children who have no control.
5. I do not have time to use this, there's just not enough time for it in the situations I am going through.
6. Well, this is the same as I-messages.
7. This is just self-indulgent selfishness.
8. This cannot be used in real situations, not with my husband/manager/child/friend/mother, etc.
9. Children need boundaries.
10. You do not know the "game plan." It's completely different game rules that apply out there!
11. You are not exactly a role model when it comes to communication.

When you get into right-and wrong thinking

To deal with this dilemma, it helps if you are clear about the difference between "moral judgments versus judgments based on values "(13) and" natural versus habitual "(14).

Behind every judgment there are beautiful needs.
Marshall Rosenberg[3]

If a dialog is focused on who did right and wrong, or at finding a scapegoat when something has gone wrong, I try to stop and listen. At this point I know a lot of listening, a big heart and a big dose of empathy will be of use. I remind myself that behind all this there are universal needs, and then it becomes easier to listen and try to create connection. It's almost like being a detective who curiously turns every stone to find clues. A participant in a leadership training I led said, after having received a lot of feedback from the rest of the group:

I realize now that as soon as I experience strong emotions I begin to look outside myself for who to blame it on.

When we explored this further, he and the others in the group discovered that we could listen to what is going on within us in a different way. We can notice what we feel and connect our feelings to our needs, instead of to thoughts about what others have done wrong. Once we have done so, it becomes easier to realize what we want to ask others about and what we want to ask ourselves about. When we stop blaming our emotions on others we have more strength to handle the situation. We can now devote ourselves to what we have a lot of possibility to influence - our own inner world - and less about what we do not have power over - what other people want and do.

I think many people will recognize themselves in this. When everything is going well we can communicate in a way that we are proud of. But as soon as we feel strong emotions our old habitual scapegoating starts. As a leader, I can use my own skills to listen and try to understand what those who are looking for right and wrong really need. I can also get help from other members of the group depending on their level of knowledge, confidence and how well they know each other.

---

3. Rosenberg, Marshall (2007), *Nonviolent Communication, a language for life.* Puddle Dancer Press.

When Someone Ridicules what you are Talking About

To deal with this dilemma, it helps if you are clear about the difference between "fear of authority versus respect for authority" (key differentiation 20) and "life-alienated versus life-connected" (key differentiation 16).

> *All truth passes through three stages. First, it is ridiculed. Second, it is violently opposed. Third, it is accepted as being self-evident.*
> Arthur Schopenhauer[4]

Schopenhauer's assertion above has been a support to me when someone has been joking about NVC or other subjects that I have shared as a teacher. When we first hear about something new that does not conform to our old world we tend to resist it.

It is also easy to make fun of new and unfamiliar ideas. I have often seen this when people first learn NVC. For example, we have the help of the four components to work out how we can express ourselves. These are easy to make fun of and to make sound comical. In the breaks I've heard people laughingly say;

*When I see ... I feel ... as I have a need of ... and I would like..."
And they fill in the dotted lines with all sorts of crazy things, for example: When I see you blow your nose, I feel sad because I have a need of cycling and I was wondering if you want to use my toaster to go to work tomorrow.*

Earlier, I felt anxious, embarrassed and annoyed when I heard this kind of joking. Now I see it more as a sign that learning is taking place and that people need to integrate and to question the new and not just take it blindly. I have confidence that after people have ridiculed something, they may be more ready to take in what suits them.

---

4. Arthur Schopenhauer. Source http://www.quotationspage.com/quote/25832.html 281212

When You Are Not Sure of Your Next Step

To deal with this dilemma, it helps if you are clear about the difference between "power with versus power over" (key differentiation 5) and "compromise versus shift "(key differentiation 16).

If you have more than a few hours with a group it may be an advantage to involve participants in influencing the content. Inviting them to do this is an opportunity to try to take joint decisions with the help of NVC. For example you can express the following requests:

"Now I need some help to see what the next step might be, I would like to see a hand up for all of you who want to continue to X." And then, "I see about half of your hands up. Now I would like to hear from two of you who do not have your hand up about what you would like to continue with. Anyone willing?"

Once you have received this information, you go on to find out what could meet most needs. If I invite a group to do a process like this, I also usually take the opportunity to clarify that the purpose of NVC is to communicate in such a way that considers everyone's needs. We are not looking to do or say the right thing, but to create opportunities to meet as many needs as possible.

In almost every opportunity such as that I get feedback that people learn a lot from these decision-making processes in the group. And yet other people express frustration that it takes so much time, especially in groups where the participants do not have training in how to express themselves in the moment when they want to make requests that we do something else. The frustration grows and when they finally express themselves it sometimes creates more of a mess. As a leader I can contribute by giving support both to the people who are experiencing frustration with the process, and those who really want to base their decisions on the needs of all having been listened to and taken into account. It may for example be handled by one part of the group continuing the dialog, while another part of the group does something else. Just to come up with that kind of decision can be a boost for the teams' confidence in that they are capable in accommodating everyone's needs.

When you have inner conflicts

To deal with this dilemma, it helps if you are clear about the difference between "self-empathy versus acting out, repressing or wallowing in feelings"(key differentiation 23) and "vulnerability versus weakness"(key differentiation 21).

The ability to listen to yourself with empathy may be of great help during a presentation or training. For example, you may need empathy if you as the leader find that you are starting to:

- judge yourself or the participants, (Aloud or silently within yourself)

- blame yourself or the participants, (Aloud or silently within yourself)

- put labels on yourself or the participants, (Aloud or silently within yourself)

- compare yourself with the participants, (Aloud or silently within yourself).

When I listen to myself with empathy, I focus on the same things as when I listen to others. First I acknowledge for myself what judgments or demands I am making of myself or of another. When I have done that, I focus on hearing the needs behind them and what I am feeling.

Since it rarely works to "push away " strong enemy images and self-criticism, it is more beneficial if you embrace these thoughts and reformulate them into feelings and needs. Once you've done this, it will be possible for you to concentrate on your presentation again or to express what is going on inside of you. You may also have gained greater clarity about how you can contribute to the group. This describes the internal process that I choose to go through to deal with what is happening.

I can, of course, also choose to ask others for support. It can be a person who is not part of the group or someone who is. Whether you ask the group to listen to you with empathy or not depends on many factors. For example, how much time you will be spending together; how much time you have already spent together; your ability to manage their reactions; their ability to respond to you with empathy and so on.

Something that can also help you in focusing on your presentation again is to remind yourself why you want to share NVC. When your goal is clear it usually also clarifies whether you want to express what is going on within you or to continue without doing so. To have an effective way to "talk to oneself" is an invaluable tool for a trainer. You can recover your ability to self-empathize, with the exercises in Chapter 2.

On many occasions I have heard people say that they really learn something when things that are "real" are expressed during a presentation or training. In addition many have appreciated hearing what is going on in someone who is in the leadership role.

When You Find Yourself "Selling" or "Preaching"

To deal with this dilemma, it helps if you are clear about the difference between "power with versus power over" (key differentiation 5) and "request versus demand" (key differentiation 11).

Community and hope are some needs that are often found behind selling or preaching. They are needs that are important to try to meet in some way. Many of us feel a lot of hope when we come across NVC, because we have finally experienced that effective communication and connection are possible. We may then get tempted to "preach" about it, instead of making use of it when we communicate.

Many encounter NVC for the first time when they attend a workshop. At NVC-trainings the participants explore how they can communicate in different situations and most of them are interested in hearing feedback on their way of expressing themselves. It is easy to expect the same interest in communication in situations with people in other settings. Therefore, as a trainer I usually warn those who attend a training not to behave as an "NVC - police" after the training. By "NVC police," I mean continuing to point out when people are expressing themselves in ways that do not create connection, or by pointing out what does not match the principles of NVC, criticizing or giving communication advice, when people have not asked for it.

It is easier to connect with others and maybe contribute to them if you use the process, than if you preach about its benefits. If they want to know about NVC and you share how NVC has contributed to you, at the same time as you give the listeners room to evaluate if NVC suits them or not, you will help people experience more choice in your connection.

It is sometimes a challenge balancing our enthusiasm for something that has been meaningful for us, with holding people's sense of choice in regard. We can be excited at the thought, "If only more people would use NVC, the world would look different." It is then easy to begin to point out when others are not expressing themselves in accordance with the principles of NVC. Perhaps even in ways that complicate the connection between you both, rather than in helping it. If people are expressing labels, judgments, comparisons and demands, we might feel tempted to tell them how they "should" express themselves. Frustrated, we loudly exclaim things like, "There are no musts," "That is an interpretation" or "manipulated is not a feeling."

If the other person becomes offended or irritated, we become perhaps even more insistent in our attempts to teach them something (even if they are not interested in it). They might sound something like this.

I am not responsible for your feelings. Your feeling of irritation is due to your not being in contact with those of your needs that are not being met. It really depends on you listening more to your assessments than to your needs.

One problem with this way of using your knowledge, is that it most likely will thwart the purpose of NVC, to create connection. Most likely it will not inspire others to want to learn more about NVC, which perhaps was one of your hopes.

You can never force anyone to use or learn NVC. The more force someone else experiences, the more likely it is that they will lose their interest in learning anything. We all have the need to choose what we put our time and energy into.

When someone is Crying or Expressing Anger

To deal with this dilemma, it helps if you are clear about the difference between "stimuli versus cause" (key differentiation 12) and "vulnerability versus weakness" (key differentiation 21).

Since NVC can affect people emotionally, it might mean that someone occasionally starts crying. Usually, I give that person attention and listen to him or her with empathy. There may be times when it is more fruitful to focus attention to others in the group. I can, for example, turn to someone who seems embarrassed when someone is crying and ask something like this.

How is it for you to see that someone is crying in the group, how does it affect you?

When I ask that question of someone else rather than of the person who is crying, the pressure might ease off the person who is crying. It can also lead to a very fruitful conversation about the space there is for feelings in the group.

When There Are Conflicts In the Group

To deal with this dilemma, it helps if you are clear about the difference between "Observations versus observations mixed with evaluation" (key differentiation 15) and "Interdependence versus dependence or independence" (key differentiation 15).

As a trainer or teacher you are sometimes confronted with situations where it is valuable to be able to mediate. Participants may find themselves in conflicts that they might want help in sorting out. Seeing conflicts being handled in the group can increase feelings of security and confidence.

When a group resolves a conflict it is a golden opportunity to clarify the principles and key differentiations in NVC. Be careful not to use a live situation as an example for learning without having ascertained that it's okay for those involved. For some people, and in some situations, it may be a very sensitive experience to be used as a "guinea pig." My general experience is, however, that it is often fine, and that many in the group will be relieved when they understand that their conflict actually contributed to the group.

Simply put, my role as a third party is to try to facilitate discussion between the conflicting parties. With the help of NVC I do so by providing support to make the observations, feelings, needs and requests of each party clear.[5]

When People Do Not Experience Their Participation as Voluntary

To deal with this dilemma, it helps if you are clear about the difference between "Choice versus submission or rebellion" (key differentiation 7) and " Empathy versus sympathy " (key differentiation 3).

If I lead a presentation or training where the participants have been asked by, for example, their boss to attend, I assume that there may be participants who are not experiencing the participation voluntarily. The more the participants experience freedom of choice, the more they will get out of participating. Imagine that you are attending a presentation because you think you should and then you hear someone talking about how one of the basic ideas of NVC is to experience freedom of choice!

---

5. Read more about how to mediate conflicts using NVC, in my book on mediation. Larsson, Liv (2010). *A Helping Hand Mediation With Nonviolent Communication*, Friare Liv.

If it feels difficult to create connection with someone or a whole group, it can be an experience of demands or obligation that has gotten in the way. Who invited you and who pays your fee will have an impact on whether your participation is perceived as a free choice or not. If it is their employers who have organized the training, the employees can easily imagine that they have no possibility of saying no. They might attend because they are worried about the consequences of not attending, rather than because they are really interested in the content.

As long as people hear demands, they can really only act in two ways. They can rebel and go against the demands they hear, or yield and submit to the demands. People who experience demands can ostentatiously sit quietly to protect their need for autonomy. When people experience freedom of choice, they tend to see more opportunities in the handling of a situation.

In every moment you have some choice of how to act. Nobody can make you do anything, but saying no is sometimes challenging. Here are some strategies you can use to handle a situation with a person who does not see a choice.

- you can meet the person with empathy and confirm that you hear that they want to have a sense of choice and autonomy.

- you can listen to the person with quiet empathy.

- you can express how it affects you that they are not connected to a sense of choice.

- You can invite them to have an open dialog about choice and autonomy and about why they are there anyway.

- you can use the situation to distinguish some important key differences regarding choice and duty.

- you can help them see where they put the responsibility for their actions and if there are more meaningful approaches.

- you can ask those who really do not want to be there to leave.

- if they say they cannot leave because they might be sacked, you can have a conversation about motivation. (If they leave the training, you might need to have a conversation with the person who hired you or is paying their wages).

When the participants are 'talking about' rather than practicing

To deal with this dilemma, it helps if you are clear about the difference between "Choice versus submission or rebellion" (key differentiation 7) and of "Persisting versus demanding" (key differentiation 18).

If a group is stuck, talking about a situation they have decided to practice on, rather than practicing to manage it, there can be several causes. It may be because the person who initiated the role play is experiencing strong emotions of some kind and needs to be heard with empathy before she or he is ready to move on. Another cause may be that the instructions are not clear to the group members or that the task is perceived as too difficult. Sometimes it is difficult to practice because of ongoing power struggles within the group, or because one or the participants feels too vulnerable to be open about things.

To help participants not to get stuck in "talking about" something instead of practicing it, there are some things you can do:

1. Give very clear instructions on what everyone in a small group is to do. Show them exactly what you want them to do.
2. Give them a short time to practice and ask them to always tell how the exercise went when they return to the big group.
3. Make it clear you are there to support them when they practice in small groups.

4. Clarify why you want them to practice and not to talk about the situation. Describe the difference and value of beeing able to talk about things in first, second and third person. It is not more important to practise than to talk about, and at the same time, part of the strenght of NVC is that there are tools we can become more skilled at using.

5. Change the grouping as often as possible at the beginning of a class.

When Someone Wants to be sure of Confidentiality

To deal with this dilemma, it helps if you are clear about the difference between "vulnerability and weakness"(key differentiation 21) and "interdependence versus dependence or independence"(key differentiation 15).

During the second day of a work-shop, a participator (with irritation in her voice) raise the issue about confidentiality.
- *We should have talked about confidentiality at the beginning of the training! I do not feel safe now at all to express myself in the group, so I am not going to share anything that is going on within me.*

Her statement provided impetus for many different reactions in the group. Unfortunately, most of the reactions did not meet her needs of respect and security. One reaction was:
You should be confident that we would not spread anything you express, even if we have not made a rule about it. What kind of people do you think we are? (This person heard her statement as a criticism.)

I certainly have nothing to hide so you can tell anything about me. (The sarcasm in this statement might have been this person's expression of the need to be seen and of trust.)

We need to be able to trust each other without having to make rules about it. Let's trust that we want the best for each other. (Again, maybe it was this persons need for trust, which was stimulated.)

After the first little "uproar" had subsided, we went back to the womans request for confidentiality. When she had been heard with empathy for what it meant to her and what needs she wanted to meet with it, she found a new way to express herself:

When I think about what I might say about my relationship with my sister, I feel vulnerable and afraid. For although I love her very much, I also find some sides of her enormously difficult. I want to feel safe in exploring all of my judgments, my annoyance, guilt and shame, without fear that it will reach back to her in a way that would damage our relationship. Is there anyone who wants to tell me how this is for you to hear?

While the first thing she had said, aroused opposition, the second brought compassion. Many in the group were amazed at how different their emotional reaction was the second time. Several expressed thanks for this, as they began to understand what compassion is all about. That it does not come from doing our duty towards someone, but from the joy of contributing to other people's lives and enabling us to see what difference this can make. Their initial reactions (criticism, sarcasm and so on) shifted when they came into contact with their having the power to enrich another persons life.

The woman felt pleased to hear that the others had no desire to tell anyone else something about her. She told me after the class that it was the attitude and connection with the others, which gave her the confidence she needed.

If You are Hired Under a "False Flag"

To deal with this dilemma, it helps if you are clear about the difference between "Choice vs. submission or rebellion" (key differentiation 7) and "empathy versus sympathy" (key differentiation 3).

As a leader in an already existing group, you had better be prepared to deal with "old sourdoughs," things that the group has not sorted out earlier and which can affect what happens today. When you meet a group within an organization, their shared background affects how what you share with them is received.

Once I was involved in a learning situation where on the very same day as I was going to lead an introduction to NVC at their workplace, everyone, without my knowledge, had been dismissed from their job. It was a very strange atmosphere and I tried everything possible to make a connection with them without results.

After a while a woman quietly began crying and I asked the group to take a break, so I could spend some time with her. Only then did I hear what had happened. The time we had left was, of course, spent on the feelings, thoughts, judgments, etc. that came up in relation to their having been dismissed. If I had been informed of this before I met the group I probably would have been able to contribute in a very different way to the participants.

The situation taught me to make sure I find out what is the background to my being asked to lead a group or training. There are many ways to do this and one is to be clear about what those who hire you expect from you.

I also ask how the participants are related to each other, if they work together and so on. If an invitation with information about what is going to be addressed during the time I'm with the group is sent out, I ask to get a copy of it. This is a way to know exactly what information the group has received (at least in writing). Often I write a suggestion of what an invitation should include, with information that can be supportive for participants. I also ask to be informed if conditions change in any way. Some people appreciate getting reading suggestions.

I have also heard of other trainers and coaches who have been hired under a "false flag" or where conditions have changed after the invitation. Often it has been about a hope that a prolonged conflict would be handled without having to name it.

When You Do Not Interrupt Although You See That It Would Make a Difference

Sometimes it is - for various reasons - a challenge to interrupt though you see that it would make a difference. One of the reasons is that we have been told it is impolite to interrupt. This makes it uncomfortable to intervene even if you guess it would be the best choice in order to support a person or a group. Learning how to interrupt and at the same time show care and warmth is a very worthwhile skill to practice. We don't want to interrupt to shut someone down, we do it because we want to support and care for connection.

A person that is talking at length is often not as disturbed by being interrupted, at least not if we can communicate what our purpose for interrupting is. We might interrupt and ask someone to clarify something, or we might say that we want to reflect back to them what we have heard to make sure we understood what they wanted to let us know. After having done it a few times it often becomes easier as you see how it can support communication. We can also say that we are curious to hear how others feel about what they have just shared and therefore honouring their input, but giving space for others to speak. If we have a sense of connection with the person we might even tell them that we are feeling a bit disconnected and want to know how they are feeling at the moment.

Use the exercise on next page to make your inner process when it comes to interruption more clear to yourself.

Exercise - Reflections On Interrupting With Empathy

1. Imagine a situation where you would like to interrupt someone who is talking. Something you've been through that you experienced as a challenge or something you think would be a great challenge for you. What exactly do you hear someone say and in what way?

2. What do you feel at the thought of interrupting?

3. What needs are not being met by continuing to listen without interrupting?

4. Which of your needs, do you think could be met by an interruption?

5. Which of your needs are you worried would not be met by interrupting?

6. What needs do you think the person who is talking is trying to meet by talking?

7. Which of the person's needs might be met by your interrupting?

8. What need might the person find it difficult to meet if you interrupted?

9. Now imagine that you interrupt by:

a. guessing the needs you think the person is trying to meet through talking about this (5). It might sound something like:

I want to understand, are you talking about this because you really want something to change?

Or,

Are you worried that what you believe is important to you is not going to be heard and received.

b. By expressing your own needs (3) "I find myself feeling a bit scattered. On the one hand, I understand this is important for you and on the other hand, I would find it more meaningful to talk about what to do with X, do you mind if we shift our focus to that?

c. What feelings and needs do these two options awaken?

d. What learning can you have from this when it comes to interrupting?

Chapter 5

Amongst Jackals and Giraffes - Role plays and Dialogs

Jackals and Giraffes

Learning is the greatest game of life, and the most fun! All children know this when they are born. They continue to believe it until we convince them that learning is hard and unpleasant work. Some children never learn that lesson but really go through life in the belief that learning is fun and the only game that deserves to be played. We have a name for such people - we call them geniuses![1]

Glenn Doman

What Giraffes have to do with Nonviolent Communication

Sometimes NVC is called "giraffe language." This is in contrast to language that does not directly focus on connection which is called "jackal language". The man behind NVC, Marshall Rosenberg, often used them in trainings. In some countries the jackal changed into a wolf or a snake.[2]

Since most people are well trained to think in terms of right and wrong, it is easy to assume that the two terms when paired together automatically means that one is right and the other one is wrong. The use of the two symbols is in this case intending to facilitate learning, not to show that one is right and the other is wrong.

The giraffe is used as a symbol of language that more easily leads to connection. The jackal is used as a symbol of a language, usually habitual, that is more challenging in creating connection.

Some trainers use hand puppets to support how communication can either create connection or contribute to distance. One hand-puppet is a giraffe and the other is a jackal. To further facilitate learning, trainer also use a headband with jackal and giraffe ears on them.

One advantage of using hand puppets is that you get access to at

---
1. Vos & Dryden (2005) *The New Learning Revolution*. Network Educational Press Ltd
2. There are clips on Youtube where Marshall Rosenberg uses hand puppets as well as a headband to demonstrate communication.

least two "personalities" to act upon, the one of the hand puppet, and your own. Using hand-puppets, or the headband, allows two people to role play different situations using NVC models of communication. This creates some separation between the "actors" and the roles played, allowing the participants in the role playing more freedom to express themselves.

Another advantage is that some people act and communicate more freely and openly with a hand puppet than they do directly with you or another person. Often the participants have a lot of fun and even very serious dialogs can be lightened up through the role play and difficult issues brought up to be dealt with.

The hand puppets also make it easier for people to remember what they have learned because they give a clear, visual picture of the situation. Examples become clear and the memory image that is created can facilitate remembrance of the vocabulary and the approach in the future. They can also make the characters more clear because they dare to "live out" the interaction more fully as they are depersonalized.

A disadvantage in using these tools can be when some people regard play and hand puppets as "not being serious." They may feel uncomfortable being invited to "talk to a puppet," therefore be sensitive about it. Be prepared to change your working method if it gets in the way of clarity about what you want to contribute to. I've even heard people who have ridiculed other participants that have appreciated hand puppets as a learning tool. If this is not handled sensitively it may grow into a bigger conflict.

In some situations I have seen people taking the opportunity to say things that can be painful for others in the group to hear, when they have been able to tell it "as a puppet" or "to a puppet." These situations may sometimes take lots of time and energy to sort out.

I often hesitate using the jackal as a symbol because I am afraid it might contribute to further demonizing those already so disparaged animals. Therefore I am always careful to clarify that we are using symbols to facilitate learning but also that it is not about right or wrong, but simply two different ways of expressing ourselves. I often refrain completely from using these symbols, however my experience has shown that the advantages for many peopel outweigh the disadvantages.

What The Jackal Puppet and Jackal Ears Can Contribute To

- Provide an opportunity to see the human side of a "jackal" and how we can create connection even with people we see as our enemies.
- Give an opportunity to practice communication in challenging situations.
- Clarify what can get in the way of connection.
- Increase the capacity for empathy, as they also contribute to the understanding of what lies behind your own use of "jackal language."
- Can provide an understanding of how "jackal behavior" can shift, if it is treated with empathy or vulnerable honesty.
- Provide an opportunity to anchor that knowledge in situations that are touching and important.
- Can lighten up situations and bring humor to facilitate learning.
- Show how our inner dialogs affect our other dialogs.
- Give a chance to show how jackal language can also create connection if that is our intention.
- What The Giraffe Puppet and Giraffe Ears Can Contribute To
- Can demonstrate challenging communication situation in a clear way.

- Provide practice in meeting someone with empathy.

- Clearly demonstrate the classic giraffe while clarifying that it is not the way we encourage people to talk.

- Enable "screaming in giraffe" with less risk of the participants taking offense or feeling insecure.

A Jackal With Giraffe Ears

There is an additional tool for use by combining the jackal hand puppet with a pair of giraffe ears, that we put on the jackal. The following points describe some of the situations where it can contribute.

- When we want to show how someone who does not communicate using NVC can empathize. For example, we can take the role of a person that it is a challenge for someone to connect with, to show in the role play how they can communicate. Taking reverse roles gives new perspective and can give hope.

- When somebody is stuck in painful communication patterns.

- When we want to make it clear that a jackal is no more than a giraffe with a language problem.

- When we want to show how we can listen to our inner jackal.

Both Hand Puppets At The Same Time

- Using both hand puppets at the same time can be of special help:

- To demonstrate a dialog.

- To demonstrate self-empathy.
- To help participants to continue a role play where they are stuck.
- To clarify a particular concept.

Role playing - some ideas of how to do it

As part of a presentation, role play can be used to clarify some parts of NVC. Role playing can contribute to both learning and understanding. It can also help workshop participants gain trust and energy to reconcile with painful events. It is also a way to practice an often-occurring situation, as role play can make it easier to transfer their skills to a situation in everyday life.

In a role play, you can "go the whole hog" because it is not the real situation. Let the participants try different responses in a situation, exaggerate, have fun, slow down; whatever support learning. Show different ways of expressing and listening to help discover what supports the connection.

You can practice with predefined roles or use examples from the participants. Some people learn a lot from participating and some learn more by observing and listening. Because of this, people may differ in their willingness to participate. Be aware of any student who feels very uncomfortable with participating in a role play. If someone does something because they feel forced to do so, it will probably be counterproductive.

Role playing can lead to different kinds of understanding and skills depending on which role you are taking. When role play is used to clarify the principles and assumptions of NVC, it is best if one of the participants is actively taking the role of the one that uses NVC and the other one might be a jackal.

Before the role playing starts, it is important to point out that you will be focusing on the connection between the two roles and not on any concrete results. Make it clear that the role-play does not necessarily have to result in a solution of, for instance, a conflict. Note that if you spend 15 minutes in a role play - having a dialog that in reality could take two hours - you will probably not come to an authentic finish. The role play is mainly a way to show how we can establish connection and to gain understanding of how communication between people can work and not a way to reach concrete solutions.

Allow yourself to bring the tempo down and take the time necessary to find new ways to express yourself. If you notice that a role play does not feel meaningful, there may be several reasons. One is that the difficulty level is too high, so it feels hopeless to reach any kind of connection. Sometimes those who are role playing think that it will be more "real" if the process of finding connection and communication are not immediately reached.

My experience is that communication in a role play, often has a higher degree of difficulty than a conversation in real life would have. The challenge level might also be too low, so that it is not found to be meaningful to practice.

Anyone who plays that role can reduce the challenge level by including more of what he or she imagines are the feeling and needs of the person they are role playing. The person who makes the presentation can also take a more active role in the role play and thus control the degree of challenge. Remind each other that this is a role play, not a real life conversation so feel free to change how things are said and heard. Another way to provide more meaningfulness in a role play is to change roles, who is playing whom and with what attitude.

As Part Of the Role play Somebody May:

a. Act as him or herself, without having to think about doing it in a certain way or in line with the principles of NVC.

b. Act as a person he or she finds it difficult to communicate with and challenging to understand.

c. Act as oneself and really try to use all his or her NVC-skills.

d. Act as the other person attempting to use NVC (Whether or not this person in real life actually knows anything about NVC).

e. Ask someone else to do some of the above while the person that presented the situation is not taking part but observes someone else role playing.

Different types of role play

Role play A-E: Person 1 chooses a role play of a situation in which she or he is involved.

Role play	Person 1	Person 2 or 3
Role play A	Takes the role of her- or himself, using their NVC-skills.	Person 2 takes the role of the other person. Communicates in any way she or he likes or find meaningful in the situation.
Role play B	Takes the role of her- or himself, communicating in any way.	Person 2 takes the role of the other person using their NVC-skills.
Role play C	Takes the role of the other (the person that person 2 role plays in version A and B). Communicates in any way she or he likes or that might support learning.	Person 2 takes the role of person 1 using NVC-skills.
Role play D	Watches the role play being played out by persons 2 and 3.	Person 2 takes the role of person 1 using NVC - skills. Person 3 - someone who has not been active in the role play so far - communicating in any way she or he likes or sees fit.

Role play	Person 1	Person 2 or 3
Role play E		We choose a situation where we role play some people that we would like connection with. Their roles are played by anyone that wants to take part and they might rotate after some time.

When the different types of role plays are useful:

I use role play A to give a person who is facing a challenge a chance to practice dealing with it.

I use role play B to give a person in pain a chance to be met with empathy. It might help them repair their trust in the other person. It can open up a willingness of wanting to communicate with this person in real life.

I use role play C when I want to help person 1 see the humanity in the other person. This often occurs when person 1, in the role of the other person, regards reality from the perspective of the other person. Role playing in this kind of situation can contribute to both inspiration and healing.

I use role play D when I think that clarity will be greater when people who participate in the role play are not strongly emotionally activated by the situation (as the people that suggested the role play are).

I use role play E to explore a topic or a dialog we are interested in learning about. We may also use this form if no one wants to bring up a personal example but we want to learn about communication on a particular topic.

Here is an example of how to set up for a role play:

1. The first step is for the person who brought up the situation (person 1) to describe the different parties. It might sound something like this.

   a. I bought something that turned out to be broken.

   b. I went back to the store to exchange it.

   c. It is five o'clock on Friday afternoon and I am in a hurry to go home.

   d. The cashier says, "how can I be sure that you did not break it yourself? we don't sell broken things."

Person 1 tells us more background information only if it is essential for the other person's ability to take the role. Avoid trying to describe the whole situation, instead simplify the description as much as possible. It can actually often help the others (person 2 and maybe 3) to take their parts if they have not heard too much from person 1.

Prepare yourself for role plays

This is a reflective exercise if you feel unclear or uncertain about using role playing in your trainings or when and how to do it. It will help you gain clarity on what kind of role play is best suited for the situation you want to role play. Use the text from the last pages as inspiration in answering the questions below.

After having used role play a few times, it will be easier for you to decide which type of role play best fits, and when. Choose the first set of questions if you are pretty new to doing trainings that includes role plays and the second if you have tried it and was not fully pleased with the result.

1a. Think about some situations where you have led or participated in a role play. Start with selecting one when you were very confident that the role play helped someone who took part in it.

b. Chose a time when you felt that it did not do so.

c. Briefly describe both situations and compare them.

2a. Describe what you think worked.

b. Describe what you think was not working.

c. What could you do differently in situations when the role play does not seem to have the effect you want?

Recovering from an unsuccessful role play

Even if role playing is usually a great way to create learning, it sometimes just doesn't seem meaningful. It might even leave you with fear or hesitancy to try it again. Whatever the reason for that is, take some time to reflect over the role play that you were not fully pleased with.

1. Pick a situation and write down all the thoughts and judgments that come up around it. Let if flow for some minutes without censoring.
2. Read what you have written and notice if there is something that sticks out, hurts or catches your attention in a particular way.
3. Is the stimuli something that someone else said or did or something you yourself said or did?
4. What are you feeling and needing, once you have found out what stimulated the pain?

5. Can you see a role play in the future where you can take care of those needs (4) in a better way?

6. Can you come up with any requests for yourself or someone else that you want to remind yourself of making before starting off a role play again?

Chapter 6

Need based Leadership

Need based Leadership

"A leader is best, when people are hardly aware of his existence.
Not so good when people praise his government.
Less good when people stand in fear.
Worst, when people are contemptuous.
Fail to honor people, and they will fail to honor you.
But of a good leader, who speaks little.
When his work is done, his aim fulfilled,
the people say, 'We did it ourselves.'"
Lao-Tse, 500's BC[1]

Being in touch with my needs is the main tool I use in getting information of how I want to lead a group. This has become increasingly more important the more I learn about leading workshops and facilitating group processes. Being connected to my own needs helps me stay connected to the group I'm leading as I don't get as easily distracted.

To be able to listen to both the needs of the group members as well as my own, contributes to my ability to determine how I want to lead a group to achieve it's goals. As a leader, I very often use the skills I have acquired through studying Nonviolent Communication - NVC. For example - my knowledge about how to listen emphatically makes the feelings, needs and requests of others more obvious to me. Listening to myself with empathy and being able to express my needs in an honest way to the group I lead is another invaluable tool. Empathy is a prerequisite for democracy and therefore the core of every group that wants to use all the resources in the group.

When we make mistakes as leaders it is essential to mourn our mistakes in an efficient manner. We all make mistakes, especially if we dare to take the risk of trying to create something new. It is essential to be able to rise again after a mistake without becoming hard or cold. Through the self-empathy process as proposed in NVC, I have learned to give myself support after making a mistake

---
1. http://www.inspirationalspark.com/leadership-quotes.html

and to better manage my "inner critic." I have also learned that I often need support when acting in a leadership role, to handle challenging situations in a way that I like.

After sharing the principles of NVC for over 10 years it was clear to me that I best support a group when I adapted my leadership style after how matured the group was. As a leader, I often ask the following questions to create clarity for myself:

- What needs are important to pay attention to in this group right now?
- In what ways can these needs be met?
- How can I use myself and my own feelings and needs as a tool to help the group to mature?
- What is the group's energy directed to? How can I support it being more focused on the goal of the group?
- Are the key issues in the group being addressed?
- What needs need to be met for the group to develop?

Leadership & Key Differentiations

In the literature about leadership and in management trainings there is much discussion about which mode or style of leadership that is most appropriate. The answer varies somewhat over the years and also depending on the context of the discussion. The leadership qualities listed below have repeatedly been considered important.

It is valuable for everyone in a leadership position to understand the four components of NVC: observation, feeling, needs and present request. I have therefore compared qualities often talked about as "leadership qualities" to create more clarity.

Qualities that are often valued in a leader:
1. Logical, (realistic, factual).

2. Human, (open, honest, empathetic).

3. Engaging, (inspiring, motivating, encouraging).

4. Goal-oriented, (action-oriented,).

These descriptions give people some direction but they are not sufficiently descriptive and practical to be of much use. On the contrary, they can easily be heard as demands or characteristics that are impossible to reach or qualities that are impossible to learn. However, if we relate to leadership as something we do, rather than to some qualities that we have or not have, we can start to practice and hone our skills.

Often people talk about the value of being realistic and logical, without having any clarity about what kind of actions they are referring to. Just describing qualities does not give the support we need. The list of "required qualities" may even stimulate people's doubts as to whether they will succeed in their leadership. It might result in decreased, rather than increased trust in themselves. Using NVC, we can find the tools that translate the four qualities above into concrete and doable actions. This will empower you to discover what can be done, rather than trying live up to some vague expectations of how a leader should be. I will use some key differentiations that Nonviolent Communication is based on to create clarity about this.

NVC Component: Observation.
Leadership quality: Logical, (realistic, clear).
Key differentiations: "To separate observations from interpretations and analysis" and "To separate stimuli from cause."

How To "Do" Logical (realistic, clear)?

Being logical is making a clear distinction between what is really taking place and your own judgments, interpretations and analysis of it. One of the basic components in NVC is to make a clear distinction between observations and interpretations and this is what a leader can focus on to embody the quality of "logical and clear." An observation is something that any of our senses register. It is based on what we see - but not what we think about what we see, or how we assess it. It is based on what we hear - but not on our diagnosis of the person who says what we hear, or how we judge what we hear.

Instead of calling someone "logical, realistic and clear" I would, in NVC terms, say that I hear someone express observations about what she or he is seeing or hearing, rather than express his or her interpretation or analysis of it.

When I as a leader focus on what actually happened, rather than how I judge something, I can protect both myself and the group or organization I work for from unnecessary misunderstandings and conflicts. When someone expresses interpretations in a group I, as a leader, can, with care, find out the answer to the questions:
What did you see this person do that makes you think that?
What was it you heard the others say?

It will help the group to connect, instead of getting stuck in analysis and opinions about what the other has done and ideas about right and wrong.

With the help of observations that are free from interpretations, the leader puts real facts on the table, "I have seen you sitting in the coffee room 15 minutes longer than the others for the last 2 weeks. Will you tell me what led you to make that choice?" The reaction to this question is totally different than to that of calling someone lazy or irresponsible.

NVC Component: Feeling.
Leadership quality: Human, (open, honest, empathetic).
Key differentiation: "To be able to differentiate between feelings and thoughts" and "The difference between vulnerability and weakness."

To Be a Human Leader

In 1982 I was in Rome for the first time and I visited St. Peter's Square where the Pope gave audience every Sunday. When the Pope came out and waved, I heard a couple next to me saying, "He is so human." I reacted with disdain, and thought these Americans were pretty ridiculous. But it stayed in my memory for some reason that I did not understand at the time. It was much later that I realized that what had made an impression on me was how important it was for these people to see a human being beyond his role. Then it struck me that these words were probably a sign that they experienced some kind of connection with the pope's humanity that was important to them (even if it was not important for me at the time).

Whatever leadership trend is in fashion, it is always much more appreciated than people in general believe, to hear what is going on within the leader. How many coffee breaks are spent talking about "the boss," and how she or he is doing, and why she or he has done one thing or the other. It takes a lot of our attention to perceive facial expressions, gestures and a tone of voice, which we interpret as strong emotions especially when we do not hear the person put these noticed gestures into words. This is especially true if the person has a major influence over our work or us. Contrary to our belief, leaders who can put into words what they feel and take responsibility for their feelings, help the group focus on their task. When we see strong emotions but the person says nothing about it, we often interpret it as if they are angry. An angry person can be a threat to our security and we want to be on our alert.

Often when I feel stress and do not express it with words, people misinterpret and believe that I feel anger or dissatisfaction. So I have learnt to put words to my stress and express it, especially when

I am in a leadership role. I express this to support the group and help it to put its focus on the goals and not in figuring out how I feel.

When a leader is anxious or nervous about something and doesn't talk about it, I have often heard it being interpreted as if that person is cold or distant. If we think that someone who has great influence on us does not care about us, it's easy to become cold or distant ourselves. We withdraw as we expect a punishment or harsh words.

A leader who doesn't register and express his or her feelings may miss how this is affecting the group he or she is leading. When obvious feelings are expressed in words, it leads to fewer misinterpretations and draws less attention from the collective task.

Provided, of course, that the person who expresses their feelings does not do so in order to blame or induce shame, but takes responsibility for his or her own inner world. A group or organization never works better than the relationships contained in the group or organization. An organization is based on the relationships between the people in that organization. When people act and relate to one another, they can help each other to achieve the goals they want to reach. When relationships in an organization are conflict-ridden and full of misunderstandings it will be harder to achieve common goals.

A leader who is connected to his or her feelings and needs, who understands that it is a part of being human, will contribute to a climate where people dare to show what they feel as well. The leader becomes a role model of how the members of the team can express their feelings and needs.

It is important both how the leader expresses her or his own feelings and needs, and how he or she treats others. A leader who has a well-filled supply of empathy will find it easier to meet others with empathy. When someone makes a mistake the leader can empathize with the needs they are mourning not being met and stay with the sadness and vulnerability that might bring.

When leaders understand that feelings, even of vulnerability, do not mean weakness, they will realize that expressions of feeling may contribute to connection, acceptance and trust.

NVC Component: Needs.
Leadership Quality: Engaging, (inspiring, motivating).
Key differentiations: "To separate needs from strategies," "Power with versus power over "," To separate demands from requests" and "Interdependence versus dependent or independent."

Motivating People

I have often wondered if we can truly motivate other people, and if yes, how? One of the assumptions NVC is based on is that behind all that humans do there is a desire to meet needs. When we as leaders connect to the needs and values of others, we find clarity about what is driving them. In finding out what someone needs we have a great advantage in being able to distinguish between the specific actions that a person is doing to meet their needs and the actual needs.

If people feel that they have a say in deciding how things are to be done, they become more motivated to contribute. If they can see how what they do can meet both their own and others' needs, the motivation will grow further. People enjoy making a difference.

Another assumption that NVC is based on, is that we want to contribute to others when we experience it as voluntary. When a leader expresses a request, many of us hear a demand, as we have learnt to obey authority. When we hear a demand, we have two choices, to rebel or submit. Neither one of these choices will lead to us being inspired or engaged. As a leader, it is therefore essential to distinguish demands from requests and to hold the need of having a choice high. It is also useful to be able to double check if what we asked for is a request and not a demand.

NVC Component: Request.
Leadership Quality: Goal oriented, (targeted, directive).
Key differentiations: "To separate needs from strategies" and "Persisting versus demanding."

Goal Orientation

Many meetings end with the group members having different ideas about what has been decided. A common reason is that the requests expressed have not been specific and clear enough and no one, including the leader, has pointed this out during the meeting. Sometimes it is also unclear why someone wants something done, namely what needs he or she hoped to meet by doing it. When needs are not clear it is usually more difficult to motivate the group. An important task of a leader is to keep the focus on the goal, as well as to link it to the underlying needs and values of the group.

There is often concern about both authoritarian and, in the opposite direction, "laissez-faire" leadership. Leadership based on the principles of NVC does not aim in one direction or the other. I want to be as clear as possible about what I want, and I also want to listen to and take in other people's needs.

The fourth component of NVC is to express your requests and to make it clear whom you want to do something, what you want someone to do and when you want them to do so. When I express a strategy or a request as a leader I want to make sure that my requests are heard as requests and not as demands. One way to find this out is by asking if anyone is worried that their needs will not be met by my request. Sometimes some needs are not met by my strategy and I might still not be willing to let go of what I have expressed. I can hold on to my request at the same time as I listen to the group members expressing their needs. I want to be able to show that they matter without having to give up on what I believe is the best way for the group to move forward.

If people say yes to my request, it is because it meets some need of theirs to do so and I also want to connect to that. I know that if they do it only "because the boss says so" it might lead to conflict and lowered good will. Through practicing NVC we obtain very distinct skills that help us to make decisions that include everyone's needs. As leaders, we are expressing exactly what we want and why and are always willing to change if we receive information that shows that there are more effective strategies.

The task of the leader

Directing the group's resources toward a common goal is maybe the most important task a leader has. To a great extent this is going to be easier if the needs of each participant in the group are met while striving to reach theses goals. Therefore, a group will benefit if the leader's way of leading is sensitive to the issues and needs of the individual group members. If the leader does not give space for team members to get answers to their questions, the group will develop at a slower pace. When the leader is perceived as standing in the way of something that is very important for team members they might also try to get rid of him or her.

Formal and Informal Leaders

> *A community is like a ship; everyone ought to be prepared to take the helm.*[2]
> Henrik Ibsen

The word leader is used to describe a few different functions. Sometimes it is used to describe a formal leader, who is the person we call leader. Sometimes there is talk about informal leadership. An informal leader could be described as the person who affects the group participants most. It may be a person who wants to influence the group in a certain direction and whom the group is willing to follow at that time. As a formal head I'm not necessarily a leader in the sense that I am the one who affects the group the most. If I am a formal leader, I can serve the group best if I make it clear to myself how much impact the group wants to give me.

Whether you are a formal or informal leader, you may use NVC and FIRO-theory (that I will describe later) to support your group in achieving its goals.

The challenge formal leaders often face is different from the challenges an informal leader meets. A formal leader might openly and early in a group's development be asked about what skills she

---
2. http://www.justfortheloveofit.org/inspiration

or he has to lead the group. An informal leader is often questioned during more stormy conditions without anyone calling them leaders.

Another difference is that a formal leader seldom has to negotiate to get time from the group in the same way as an informal leader does. As a formal leader you often are expected to come with some kind of proposal for how the time of the group shall be used, while informal ones often need to negotiate with the other group members to get them to agree on some particular topic.

To make people aware of this difference I express how much time I want to use for a particular issue or exercise in the group. I do it to show participants how to take more responsibility for time and energy and give them the opportunity to influence what is happening in the group both in the moment and in the future. I might say:

I would like us to use 40 minutes on this task. Is there anything that you need in order to go ahead with the first point?

As a formal leader, I notice how much more attention my ideas get, than when I introduce similar ideas as a participant of a group. Sometimes it is of course because the group appreciates my suggestions, and many times it is just because I'm seen as their leader. We are so used to "obeying" and hearing the requests of a leader as demands that many of us do not realize we have a choice of saying no when the leader makes proposals.

People in staff rooms often talk about their boss or the management, without it reaching back to her or him. As formal leaders, it is prudent to assume that the people you are leading are indeed talking about you in one way or the other and that you may be the last to know what is being said. Whether the talk is 'positive' or 'negative', it will be expressed in one way or another. Many people have underlying attitudes about whoever is in charge.

I will hold back the development of the group if I want to lead the group but the group does not want me to be the leader. Leadership is something I need to be willing to take, but also something that will work best if I receive it from the group. If I do not want to lead, but the group wants me to, this will also restrain the group.

Having a high position does not mean you are automatically a leader. There are, for example, managers who would not be able to or want to lead a group in crisis. I believe that there are many people with leading positions in organizations that are simply administrators or monitoring what is happening. Leadership is something much more dynamic and natural than the power conveyed by titles.

The "Best" Management Style

If one is truly to succeed in leading a person to a specific place, one must first and foremost take care to find him where he is and begin there.

This is the secret in the entire art of helping.

Anyone who cannot do this is himself under a delusion if he thinks he is able to help someone else. In order truly to help someone else, I must understand more than he—but certainly first and foremost understand what he understands.

If I do not do that, then my greater understanding does not help him at all. If I nevertheless want to assert my greater understanding, then it is because I am vain or proud, then basically instead of benefiting him I really want to be admired by him.

But all true helping begins with a humbling. The helper must first humble himself under the person he wants to help and thereby understand that to help is not to dominate but to serve, that to help is not to be the most dominating but the most patient, that to help is a willingness for the time being to put up with being in the wrong and not understanding what the other understands.

Søren Kierkegaard[3]

Sometimes there is a discussion about which leadership style is best, for example, what kind of boss will create the best results. As I see it the most effective leadership is based on ability to understand the critical needs of the group and to be able to serve those needs. The image of the leader as a servant, rather than as a ruler,

---

3. http://www.skmurphy.com/blog/2007/02/13/kierkegaard-on-the-art-of-helping-others-to-understand/

makes a big difference in the results of a group, especially in the longer perspective.

When I lead an NVC- training, the goals of the team are usually so-called process - or development goals. These goals are frequently changing because they are all about learning and can always be developed. As a leader I want to help the group members to focus their energy on common goals. As a leader I can do that by discussing with them whether what we do is in line with these goals or if energy is currently being used for something else. When people are not accustomed to being invited to participate in decision-making, they may find it confusing. They can then either be passive and not participate or be obstinate and rebel against everything. When people have been through this a few times and have become confident that they will be heard and can influence, but not punished if the decisions leads to some kind of failure, they usually appreciate it very much.

Learning how to use NVC in a group can sometimes take a lot of time and energy. Questions can be "put on the back burner" and the group may lose their clarity on what the purpose of the process really was to being with. While many learn a lot by being a part of processes in groups and to directly test their communication skills, there is almost always someone who has difficulties in finding lengthy group processes useful.

In some groups, members can consciously or unconsciously avoid certain subjects. And if these subjects are important for achieving the goals of the team it is often fruitful if the leader can bring in that subject.

In other groups the best support for the group is if the leader suggest every one to work towards the common goal, instead of continuing with the processing, or talking about the issue. It is sometimes uncomfortable to express these types of requests to a group that has spent time dealing with a conflict by talking but somtimes placing the issues on the sidelines for some time may actually support the group the most. It might also be seen as contradictory in some NVC groups to suggest to not continue talking.

The Charge of Leadership

Probably you have heard that migrating geese fly in a V formation. Flying in this formation allows them to increase their flight range by 70 percent because they glide more efficiently, which reduces energy expenditure. The leader breaks through the resistance of the wind, and the others glide more easily through the draft created. Flying in a V also lets the geese see ahead and may help in avoiding obstacles or bad weather and to keep coordination within the group. The geese in the formation take turns being the leader. When the current leader gets tired, he drops to the back of the formation and another moves to the front. The lead goose is not necessarily an older or stronger goose. All geese are born with the ability to navigate. If the leader chooses the wrong way, the flock will separate to quickly reform with a new leader going in a new direction. They are born with an excellent sense of direction that helps them find their way to their winter migration grounds then back to their homes.

Geese fly at different altitudes depending on conditions and purpose. In good weather, they fly at around 3,000 feet to cover the most distance they can. But to avoid bad weather, they may fly as high as 9,000 feet. They travel at speeds ranging from 40 to 60 miles per hour. They make honking noises while they fly to encourage each other to stay in the formation and keep going! There are a lot of things we can learn about how to both lead and be part of a group through studying geese as well as other animals.

"If we were only as smart as animals, we would very quickly find ways to cooperate," is a teasing statement I sometimes express in groups who are finding it hard to work together. The idea came from the observations I made during the annual stallion release I used to visit as a "horse girl" in my teens.

Knowing that it can be provocative to compare humans to other types of animals, I use the following example to highlight my thoughts about leadership. (I do not intend to make an analysis of the behavior of horses, but want to readers to create more awareness about what can help groups to improve their relationships).

On large pastures outside my hometown, colts are released together every year. A large amount of curious people come to watch the event, because they think it is exciting to see how the horses create a particular order or manage conflicts in agreeing about how to behave in the summer pasture. The first brief moment after the horses have been let out (I call this the inclusion phase[4]) they look at each other from afar and move gently around. They nibble a little grass, but many do not seem particularly interested in eating.

It does not take long before they begin to approach one another. They stretch; smell each other, gently bite here and there and run quickly, side by side, as if competing or "showing off." This moves into clashes with biting, kicking and the formation of different groups that rival each other. (I see this as the control phase *) But calmness usually occurs before night and the horses peacefully graze side by side (openness phase*).

During summer, it happens now and then that a young horse has matured and wants to measure his strength with the other stallions. When the challenges are over they move on to eat and enjoy their time together again. The ranking is to protect the herd and is not to provide advantages to the leading stud. It is functionally based and has none of the moral dilemma that arises when people try to organize themselves, with or without ranking.

A large part of our challenge is that we are so influenced by the domination system we have lived in over the past five thousand years. In systems based on domination and moral judgments, the question of leadership is charged, because leadership is seen as such an important role. The dominance system regards leadership as the most important of all social functions or roles.

In most organizations leaders and managers receive the highest .wages and the most benefits. They seem to deserve extra privileges and be entitled to greater prosperity than others. No wonder that people in such systems are ready to fight to become a leader or to try to prevent others from becoming one. We have learned that it is important to win and also to own and to have a respected position, so power struggles are very common.

---

4. See more about the terms inclusion, control and openness phase under the header "FIRO and NVC" on page 187.

The Domination System and Leadership

Our view of human nature is shaped by the society we grow up in. It is given to us by example and by our use of language. Wink[5], Hartmann[6] and Eisler[7] are some of those who have used the concept of "Domination System" or "Domination Cultures."

In different ways they have tried to describe the system based on good and bad and right and wrong, that we have created over the past 10,000 years. In domination systems the following strategies are used to maintain order: coercion, threat, punishment, reward, shame or guilt. These are systems where the few dominate over the majority to maintain control. Many of our families, schools, associations, religious congregations, companies and governments are managed in this way.

In systems based on domination, the view of human beings is often based on the idea that we are selfish and that we will do anything to achieve our own advantages. If we assume that selfishness or laziness is our true nature, then it follows that people need to be controlled so that no one harms another. In order to determine who should control whom, it is important to compare and rank humans. To keep track of who shall have the most power according to this is not easy. Through the last few millennia we have had a constant conflict over who are the good guys and who are the bad ones.

Those who are leaders in this kind of system attempt to control people using power over them. Those who obey and do what the leader wants them to do are rewarded and those who disobey are punished. With the belief that people are mainly selfish, only caring about themselves, punishment and reward appear to be effective ways of controlling people. The idea is that the punishment or being deprived of promised rewards will show that one has done something wrong. Correspondingly we understand that we are okay because those at the top (parents, teachers, managers and

---
5. Wink, Walter (2000), Powers that be. Theology for a New Millennium. Doubleday Image.
6. Hartmann, Thom (2001), The Last Hours of Ancient Sunlight Hodder & Stoughton.
7. Eisler, Riane (1987), Chalice and The Blade. HarperCollins.

others) have rewarded us in some way. We learn that our value as humans' lies in whether authorities approve us of or not. It turns us into marionettes that are easy to control.

This view of human beings justifies the idea that those who are superior have the right to rule over us; as this is the way humans learn what is right and wrong. Learning what is morally right and wrong is extremely important to be able to adapt to a system based on hierarchy and domination. Most of us are very well trained in this way of thinking. We have learned to compare and to judge what is good and what is bad, who is worse and who is better.

View Of Human Beings

When leaders choose to focus on what people need, rather than who has done something right or wrong, we increase our chances of creating a world where there is space for everyone. Such an approach is of considerable help to persons who assumes a leadership role. Having the focus on universal human needs makes it easier to see the human in each person, regardless of how they have acted. Regardless of the world around us, we can choose to have a view of human beings that suggests that all human action comes from the desire to enrich life by responding to needs.

I have seen countless examples of how we humans enjoy helping each other when we experience it as voluntary and understand how we are making a difference for someone else. It seems as if we really enjoy cooperating to meet needs if we feel like we have a choice around it. We need a sense of coherence and meaning in what we do and many of our needs are easier to meet in connection with other people.

The approach behind NVC is not dependent on beliefs about people being good or bad. It is based on human beings acting on and trying to satisfy our needs. To support this view of human beings we need to learn to communicate about what we need. We need a language that can help us to clarify the life-serving intent hidden in the learned language we use that is based on domination and control. When we do, we take a step away from a rules-based world governed by right and wrong thinking, where we blindly obey authority figures.

If I – in the role of a leader - see myself as a servant, rather than as a ruler, I will have a greater chance to contribute to creating a system based on mutual respect and freedom. Many may be used to the word "lead" and associate it to a leader who requires someone to passively follow, as a dog on a lead but that's not what I mean by leadership.

A leader is someone who serves the group by acting as a leader or a channel for resources already existing in the group. A leader is someone who is willing to give up her leadership at any moment it no longer serves the group or helps the group move towards its goal(s). Following a leader is not obedience it is a choice.

The Self-fulfilling Prophecy Of The System

The following image demonstrates how our view of human beings and the systems we create are interrelated. Every part of this circular way to describe how people and systems interact, leads to a certain result whereby everything we do becomes a kind of "Self-fulfilling prophecy." Imagine what happens in the two systems with two different ways of viewing human beings. Based on the current view of human beings, a certain kind of organization is created. These organizations require the children brought up in them to fit into serving the organizations. The way they are socialized will affect how they behave. When we see these behaviors, our view of humanity is either confirmed or changed.

This simplified way of describing the course of events is of course not comprehensive but hopefully gives a little more clarity on how our view of humanity affects the way we look at groups and leadership. Does it provide some insight into the kind of structures and leadership models you interact with?

On page 179 we considered what this cycle might look like if we shifted to a basic assumption of NVC. Different changes take place if other circles change, for instance, changes in how we structure our organizations will influence what children will be taught in school.

**View of Humanity
(or the story of our nature):**
People are lazy and selfish.

What Behavior Does This Lead To:
This socialization process will make people obedient. They will do things when they're told, threatened with punishment or promised a rewards. Some people will rebel. We judge others according to the right and wrong we have learned and hope that judgments will motivate the change we want to see.

Organizations:
Because people are lazy and selfish we need organizations that can control and motivate us. We need institutions that are controlled with the aid of carrots and sticks. These organizations need leaders who can distribute punishments and rewards to those who deserve it.

Upbringing, Education and Other Socialization:
For people to be willing to work within the organizations grounded in this system, we need to – already as children - learn to obey and to do things in the way those in power have decided. Therefore, we need schools and other organizations that educate and train us to obey, give orders, demand, punish and reward those who have earned it. Parents and teachers need to teach children what is normal, abnormal, appropriate, inappropriate, good and poorly and so on.

View of Humanity (or the story of our nature):
People do things because they want to meet their needs. They want to contribute to others if they can do so voluntarily.

What Behavior Does This Lead To:
People that have learned to listen for what they and others feel and need will listen with empathy. Because they have learned that it is possible to meet both their own and others' needs, they will try to find a solution that will meet everyone's needs as long as they experience it as a free choice.

Organizations:
If people are motivated by needs and by free choice, organizations that make it clear how and when we have met our own and others' needs, will be the ones that serve us the most.

Upbringing, Education and Other Socialization:
For people to thrive in this kind of organization it is important for them to experience and communicate their needs, instead of what they think people are or deserve. They will also learn to listen for what other people and the organization need. It takes leaders that can contribute to thinking and communicating in this way.

The Difference Between Systems Focusing on Domination and Systems (more directly) Focusing on Serving Life

To see the differences between domination systems and more life-serving systems can be helpful when we have a leadership role.

Who is Best Suited To Be A Leader?

Domination Systems	Life-serving Systems
Men have better leadership skills than women. (This means that it can be difficult to get accepted as a female leader in these systems.)	The leader may be a woman, a man or a child, depending on what serves the group the best.

The function of the leader

Domination Systems	Life-serving Systems
The leader is the most important person. The leader has the power to decide over others and is supposed to do so.	The leader is an important person, just like everyone else is important. One of the leader's most important tasks is to help the group to achieve its goals.

The role of the leader when it comes to conflicts

Domination Systems	Life-serving Systems
The leader should have control over all conflicts. Usually through pushing them away or by using power and force to stop any sign of conflict.	The leader sees and points to conflicts and tries to give support in handling them. The leader can receive help to manage conflicts and perhaps he or she steps aside if it benefits the group.

The Use of Power

Domination Systems	Life-serving Systems
The focus is on allocation of resources and power, to support cooperation among people.	Power is used to ensure that resources are allocated to those who need them the most.

The Power Of the Leader

Domination Systems	Life-serving Systems
The leader can make decisions that are not necessarily rooted in the group. He does not need to explain himself. This decision is important to obey, no matter if we know the motives behind it. The end justifies the means.	What the leader says is as important to listen to as to what any other person says. In some cases, more, if the leader has information that no one else has. The leader makes decisions to serve the group, but consults to the greatest possible extent those who will be affected by the decisions.

Resource Allocation

Domination Systems	Life-serving Systems
The leader is entitled to more resources, often in the form of money, simply with the justification that a leader deserves more.	The leader, like the rest of a group has access to the resources she or he needs to be able to serve the group.

Cooperation

Domination Systems	Life-serving Systems
Cooperation is based on duty, guilt and shame, or "us and them mentality" and often on competition with other groups	Cooperation is based on autonomy and interdependence. People want to contribute and cooperate if they can do so voluntarily and if their own needs are being considered.

Responsibilities Of The Leader

Domination Systems	Life-serving Systems
The leader is responsible for the others in the group and their needs. The leader must "take responsibility" when goals and objectives are not achieved.	Everyone, including the leader is responsible for their own and others' needs and that the group reaches its goals.

What Means Are Used To Achieve The Objectives?

Domination Systems	Life-serving Systems
Punishments and rewards are used to control peoples actions and choices.	Communication based on honesty and emphatic listening is used to influence people. Force and power can be used in immediate risk situations, but only to protect and never to punish.

Chapter 7

Need based Groups

People have lived in small groups since ancient times and there are natural processes in a group that have developed to serve us. I have chosen to describe what happens in relationships within groups with a certain theory, but I could as well have chosen another of the other great group theories that exist. The important thing for me is to try to describe stages that all groups appear to go through to understand how we can act to support groups, if we are a leader or a participant of the group. If we were studying certain flock animals, we would see similar events such as when a working group is formed.

As a leader I think it is worthwhile to bring in the idea of the group itself as a living organism that has its own dynamics. It's like in a dance where every individual has his own process and where every move affects all the others.

By a group I mean individuals with a common goal. There is interdependence between each individual and one person's choice affects all the others in some way. If the group is large -more than ten to fifteen people- it can be seen as more than one group because we cannot hold as many close relationships in consideration at the same time.

Some groups mature quickly and easily while the development of other groups takes both time and effort. Some groups never reach a functioning cooperation but are shattered. When a group receives support and challenges at a level the group members can cope with, the group matures. A group develops with the tasks it takes on. This is true unless the challenges grow and get so great that the group splits up, or diminishes so that some people will leave the group because they do not experience sufficient stimulation or that their skills are used.

FIRO – Fundamental Interpersonal Relations Orientation

A leader is the material through which energy flows with ease

Will Schutz developed a theory of human relationships which has been a great support to me as a leader. He called it Fundamental Interpersonal Relations Orientation or FIRO. Using FIRO Schultz described general human relationships in groups, so the theory is not a group theory in the strict sense.

FIRO was presented in 1958 after Schutz had been asked to investigate why staff groups with the same education achieved such different results. Schutz found that a lot of the difference in efficiency was due to the group's internal relationship and the way its members communicated between themselves.

In FIRO, three main dimensions are used to describe the relationships within and between members of a group. It gives a map to navigate processes both when you are a participant or the leader of a group. The more I have used this map, the more I see that the assumptions that FIRO and NVC complement each other. FIRO has helped me share the NVC- skills more effectively because it has supported me in understanding how and when I can intervene to support a group. The ideas behind FIRO have helped me to more easily show the members of a group in which way they are interdependent. It has also helped me to become clear about the synergies that can be achieved when we consider our relations with one another.

As I have come to understand and use FIRO, I have had more ease and effectiveness in sharing NVC with groups and helping them see their own strengths.

FIRO and NVC

Both Schutz (FIRO) and Rosenberg (NVC) attempt to describe natural processes that occur within and between people. The theories of FIRO and NVC are completely separate. I want to emphasize that the text below is my own understanding of how and in what context these theories and approaches can be used to help a group to develop.

A group is constantly changing, such as the change in its composition (someone gets invited, someone leaves) or if the goal of the group is questioned or challenged. Each group will now and then return to previous dilemmas, but if group members have gone through some challenging situations together they bring with them some experiences that can facilitate conflict resolution and thus also cooperation in the future.

When I have the opportunity to share NVC with a group for five or more days, I find it greatly supports the group if I include a presentation of FIRO.[1] I want to share the parts of the theory behind FIRO that has been of greatest help for me.

The Inclusion Phase

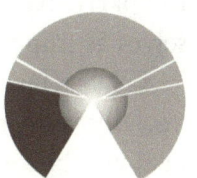

When a group is formed, we are entering the phase Schutz calls the inclusion phase. It is a phase where the participants, unconsciously or consciously, try to answer – internally - questions like;

"May I join this group?" and "Do I want to be part of this group?"

As a participant in a group we carry these questions until we have found satisfactory answers to them. If we experience a yes to the first question, we will consider the other and vice versa. If the

---

[1]. FIRO-theory as it has often been presented in Sweden has sometimes been criticized for not being faithful to the thoughts of Schutz. The most important thing for me has not been to render the theory completely, but to provide a description of events in a group that I think is a support for a leader. See also Susan Whelan's theory in order to gain more inspiration about how groups functions.

answer is no to either question, we will not fully join the group. One of my tasks as a leader is to help the members of a group to answer these questions for themselves.

Imagine a few people on a pier. A boat is moored and some people have decided that they want to travel in it and they are already sitting in the boat. The people on the pier are not quite sure if they can or want to come along. A few tentatively try to put a foot in the boat and some carefully examine whether there is room for them. Those who are already sitting in the boat politely give up their seat if anyone wants it. Some converses politely about the weather, while others are silently watching.

In a new group, most of us will be polite and not very direct in our expressions in order to make sure to support our place in the group. Some people are more open than others as a strategy of getting answers to their questions about membership. Some talk very little and focus more on listening to get to the answers.

From a need perspective, there are some needs that are particularly important to pay attention to when a new group is forming. For example, the need for acceptance, participation, security, to be seen and to experience a certain level of contact can be crucial for the participants in entering the group. We want to experience ourselves as important and experience that we have a place.

If I as a leader help the team to find new ways to meet needs, especially those above, I will help the group to develop. Group members will become more involved in working toward team goals. All our needs are, of course, important in all phases, but if you do not initially listen to the above needs, it will be more difficult to satisfy other needs that appear when the group has developed further. When everyone experiences themselves as part of the group, the issues and the questions above will be replaced with new ones.

In the Inclusion Phase the Members of the Group Often Choose to:

- Try to get to know each other
- Are very polite to each other
- Try to predict the behavior they expect of the other team members
- Ask for or demand order and structure
- take few personal risks
- Express a strong wish to experience acceptance in the group
- Express little need to connect to the group
- Rarely talk about conflicts in the group
- Try to analyze and interpret non-verbal and symbolic signals
- Demonstrate a big need to understand the team goals and ground rules
- To question their own and others' values
- Show that they depend on the leader
- Show that they are unsure whether they should or should not be part of the group
- Propose many activities for the group, few of which are followed through
- Participate in lengthy discussions on various topics that do not necessarily affect them
- May be reluctant to talk about their own potential "hidden agendas"
- Ask themselves:

Why am I / we here?
Is this the right group for me / them?
Can I / they function within this group?
Can I be myself in this group?
What will the others and I demand of me?
What rules will apply to the group?

Summary Of the Inclusion Phase

Important questions from group members:	Do I fit into this group? Do I accept the others? May I join? Am I accepted? Who are the others in the team? Do I want to be with them?
The focus of the group:	Membership (to join in or not)
Important needs:	Acceptance, safety, being seen and included, contact.
Common behaviors:	Talking about everyday things, the weather. Talking a lot. Pulls away and is silent. Asking for proof of the competence of the leader. Asking questions about the goals and standards of the group.

The Control Phase

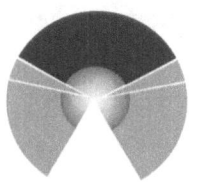

In the phase that in terms of FIRO is called the Control phase, participants will try to find their "role" in a group. The questions that will now be important for participants' will be around influence and power. The questions will be something like:

Who is leading this group?
How do I want to influence this group and what we achieve?
How will I be able to influence?

If we go back to the metaphor of the boat, everyone has stepped into the boat, (even if someone sometimes threatens to jump up on the pier again). Some people want to row to show their strength while others want to show how great they are at sailing.

Discussions about where to go are common and some are trying to get control over the rudder to steer the boat in the direction they want it to go. It sometimes ends up with the boat going round and round, or it does not move at all because of the endless discussions about goals that take all the group's energy. Fear about not being seen as competent is big, and even those who have never been in a boat might try to become captain.

The universal human needs that now falls most into focus are the needs of freedom to choose, the opportunity to influence and to use the resources of the group in a meaningful way. We want to be seen as competent and our needs of respect and dignity that are always important might become even more important. They usually go hand in hand with our desire to influence and if and how we are allowed to do so.

Now, people are generally not as cautious and polite as before. Here, people are more willing to take the risk of not being liked - or even to be thrown out from the group. But is it often a kind of "fake" independence. Conflicts arise and can be both tough and difficult to manage. Who will lead the group is an important issue to deal with and the more openness there is about this, the more effective the dialog will be.

Many people want a leader, but when someone is willing to take on the responsibility of leading the group that person is often questioned. It can be a formally appointed leader or manager, but also a person who is willing to influence, lead and take responsibility.

Vulnerable expressions

Something that helps a team to mature quickly is vulnerability (in the picture symbolized by hearts in the center of the symbol). When someone dares to take the risk of "opening up," usually more people will take this lead. In the end this kind of openness helps the group to find answers to the questions members are struggling with.

The two basic parts of NVC are honest expression of needs and listening to others. In this phase, many fear that open vulnerability would diminish the possibility to be seen as competent. There may also still be a strong fear of being expelled from the group. It is often a challenge to show oneself vulnerably in a group where it has become a norm to confront others more than expressing oneself.

When expressing vulnerability our values are revealed, which will help the group gain clarity about how participants' skills can be used in the group. When there is trust that everyone really wants to understand, it is – obviously - easier to create open and vulnerable communication. The difference between being open about what goes on inside of me versus confronting someone may depend on how we express ourselves. If I am dissatisfied with something and use a confronting way to express it, I might say something like:

I do not think it is right to act like this. What right do we have to control others!

When I am dissatisfied, I can use the principles of NVC and take responsibility for what goes on inside me, and instead express something similar along these lines, "I am concerned about the way we have solved this up till now, because I value people's freedom to choose, and do not see the possibility of it in how we are doing things. Is someone willing to tell me how this is for you to hear?"

To question the behavior of others and the team leader is something that can serve the group and help it to mature. What the result will be depends more on how the questioning is done than that it is done and how it is received. If I expose what goes on in me when expressing something that I am not happy about, it will likely contribute to the group's maturity. If I just express what I think others have done wrong it can slow down the development of the group.

As a leader with knowledge of NVC, I can benefit greatly from the ability to respond to any questioning with empathy. Whatever the form of something that is expressed, I can choose to listen for the person's feelings, needs and wants, instead of listening for what they think is wrong. I listen with the attitude that I can get more information about how to improve things, rather than listening with the attitude that someone is after me and is criticizing my way of leading.

The control phase is the most challenging for a group to mature through and it can take time to bring clarity to the distribution of power and influence. With the domination system that has been the system that has been adopted in almost all parts of the world, the difficulty in this phase increases. Sometimes people name the control phase "a power struggle" as if it is something negative or bad. If we instead see the control phase as an intensive involvement in how power and resources are allocated, it can be easier to handle. See more about this under the heading "The charge of leadership."

Something that will help the group to develop in this phase is that group members are given a task that requires a leader to solve, or that is experienced as a challenge to their skills. The same applies if the members are encouraged to discuss how the resources and expertise that exists in the group are being used and the reasons for this.

In the Control Phase, the group members frequently choose to:

- Form subgroups
- talk less about how great this group is
- demonstrate that they experience competition with each other and between subgroups
- use excuses or defenses when someone questions their behavior
- try to convince others about "the right opinions"
- show resistance to being affected by certain people in the group
- show reluctance to making decisions
- do things that can increase the frequency and intensity of conflicts
- try to take or avoid leadership
- try to resolve the disagreement or disputes by voting, compromising, or by letting someone from outside the group decide
- Actively try to expose each other's hidden motives', but rarely talk about their own
- give each other feedback based on moral judgments and demands
- Avoid showing that they have a need for acceptance in the group
- take big risks and express themselves in a way that clearly shows that they are willing to take the consequences of their actions, even if it would mean that the group does not want them
- have very different levels of activity
- say that they want more structure and leadership, but do not support it when they get it
- talk about the formal leader when he or she is not present
- try to reduce the stress caused by conflicts, by doing something completely different.

Summary of The Control Phase

Important questions from group members:	Who is the leader of the group? How much influence does the leader have? How much can I influence? Am I strong enough to stand up for what is important for me? Am I seen and respected? My competence? Do I see and respect the others?
The focus of the group:	Responsibilities and influence
Important needs:	To influence, to be heard and seen in their skills, respect, autonomy.
Common behaviors:	Trying to achieve or avoid leadership. Questioning the behavior of the leader and other group members. Comforting and trying to numb feelings. Selecting the oldest or least influential person as leader. Forming of subgroups. Performing majority voting to designate leaders.

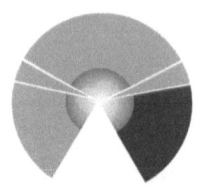

Openness Phase

When all group members have found and accepted the degree to which they want to and are allowed to influence the larger group (at least in the moment), new issues will arise. The phase that the group is now entering is called the openness phase in FIRO terminology. The group enters this phase when the main issues of values and all main conflicts have been cleared up.

Something dramatic in the leadership issue happens at this point. The role of leadership is no longer necessarily so important or loaded. The leadership may switch to the person who at that moment is most suited to lead the group. The focus here is on how to use the resources and the expertise that exists in the group. Group members recognize that they are interdependent and that everyone benefits from everyone having the opportunity to contribute. Now the group is highly effective in achieving its goals. It may mean more responsibility for all group members. But everyone will see a real reason to cooperate. Many perceive this phase as incredibly meaningful and creative. If you once have been part of a group that functions this way you will not forget it.

Now the most important questions will have to do with closeness, openness and mutual respect. We ask ourselves how much closeness and openness we want in relation to the others in the group.

The group makes room for choice, while at the same time everyone is fully aware that everything we do will influence others, which is easier than before. We will naturally and without too much trouble act in accordance with the principles that NVC is based on, mutual respect and autonomy. In addition, it is now clear that we are all responsible for how our cooperation is working and that we can achieve our common goals.

Conflicts can still occur in this phase, but they will be resolved openly because power issues are not taking over and making it more complex. Relationship problems are solved as they arise. It is easier to be vulnerable in a group where I have confidence that I have a place and trust that I'm important. This vulnerability allows things that could lead to conflict - if they were hidden - to now be "put on table "and solved jointly by the group. Happiness is no longer a personal matter. When the energy of the group is no longer being spent on questions about whether you can join or if you are allowed to influence, the group effectiveness increases.

The approach of NVC assumes that we are interdependent while at the same time we have a strong need to be recognized as free autonomous individuals. This is what mature groups experience, without even having to focus on it consciously. Many groups never reach here. This is especially true if the group is within an organization that emphasizes competition between individuals and groups. The leadership also plays a major role in whether we are achieving the openness needed for a group to develop as far as this.

In this boat people are helping each other with the chores that are needed to get the boat towards the common goal. You can see how the one who spots land contributes to the whole as well as those who are rowing. When someone at the oars becomes tired, someone else takes over. Maybe they sing or cheer on those rowing to keep their spirits up. Or they just enjoy the quietness together.

If someone gets sick the others care about that person and he or she may perhaps rest in the bow of the boat until they are healthy again. During a break some decide to swim to a nearby rocky island in order to explore if there is a place where they can anchor the boat. Some others climb up the mast to enjoy the view. When it's time to start rowing again everyone starts with his or her own job or the job they are fitted to handle.

At this phase members of the group often begin to:
- manage conflicts as they arise.
- ask others in the group for help and offer support to others.
- express that they feel safe.
- are open to suggestions of others, even if the suggestions comes from outside the group.
- express their feelings, needs and requests in a way that helps others grow.
- express appreciation for being part of the group and what the group provides.
- accept that people choose to spend different amounts of time with some of the members of the group and in smaller groups
- accept that people are active in different ways
- implement solutions based on everyone's needs or on how all needs might be met – at least consider everybody's needs
- express requests that everyone is heard, or taken in consideration
- show warmth and caring towards each other
- give energy to personal relationships within the group
- regard conflicts as common problems that provide opportunities for the group to develop
- more often have a dialog where everyone's needs are listened to before implementation of ideas
- show appreciation that things work
- manage the balance between relating (including solving conflicts) and performing their tasks
- make decisions even though there were many contradictions in the discussion about the topic that is to be decided upon
- express that they understand that everyone can do something to help the group develop
- show that they are willing to look outward to learn from the outside world

Summary Of The Openness Phase

Important questions of group members:	How open do I want to be? How strongly can I express feelings? How will I be received if I'm honest? Is there a risk I will be rejected? How is the honesty of others received? Is there warmth and caring about others? About Me? How open do we want and can we be?
The focus of the group:	Relationships (autonomy and mutual dependence in balance).
Important needs:	Mutuality, community, love, warmth, openness.
Common behaviors:	Feelings, needs and requests are expressed more openly than before. Needs are expressed more often. The physical distance decreases, increased body contact. Subgroups formed without others being disturbed about it. Openness about the various options when it comes to problem solving. Silence occurs and is not immediately broken as it is experienced as restful.

What to focus on

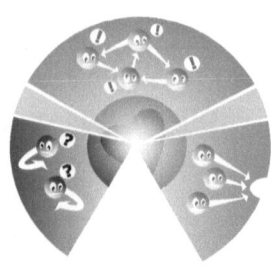

In the inclusion phase, group members generally focus inwardly. They focus on their own questions about whether they want to and may belong to the group.

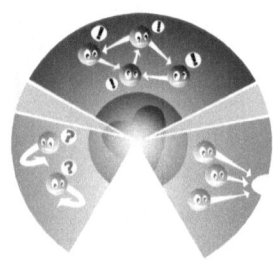

In the control phase members pay more attention to the others in the group. They question and really want to know whom it is they are letting themselves be influenced by.

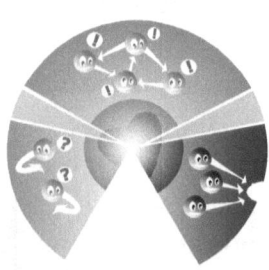

In the openness phase the members of the group are more and more focusing on the common goal. The main issues related to mutual relationships have been managed and are no longer in the way of group resources being used in reaching the objectives. The group can now connect with other groups more easily.

Leadership in the Inclusion Phase

When the group is focus on the theme of belonging, which could take anywhere from a few minutes to several years to sort out, the group benefits from a leader who gives structure and shows clear leadership. It may mean suggesting to work in smaller groups, providing clear instructions on who works with whom, giving specific instructions about what to do and about what the group will begin with. The leader helps everyone to be seen and heard in the group. For example the leader can direct questions to someone who has not said very much, or give a task to someone who has not received as much attention as others in the group. The leader helps people become visible in order to facilitate participants in a new group finding the answers to the important questions: "Do I want to be part of this group?" and "Am I allowed to join this group?."

The leader is most supportive if she or he makes it easier for group members to focus on their relations with one another because it is so central in this phase. To help everyone – or at least as many as possible – to connect and to maybe co-operate with everyone else.

Having a clear structure reduces the uncertainty in this phase, the anxiety and even the agony that characterize an immature group. It allows individuals in the group to dare to be more open and thereby contribute to the maturity and growth of the group. Leaders in the way they lead contribute to everyone's needs for affiliation and acceptance to be met. To provide simple short tasks that the group solves in small groups gives everyone a chance to be seen and involved. The main purpose of leadership here is to help the group members experience a sense of context and that they are welcome as members of the group.

Using NVC as a Leader in The Inclusion Phase

When I lead NVC-trainings, in start with giving beginning the group various short exercises, preferably in many different groupings. I try to help participants find answers to questions about their membership. The issues become easier for them to find out if they have had (at least a little) connection with everyone in the group.

I would rather "over-instruct" than be vague and leave room for interpretation. The clearer the task is, the easier it is for participants to focus on the important membership issues. Even if you as leaders is clear about what to do, it is not certain that it is clear to the group members.

Agreements and Schedule

When I meet a newly formed group, I make sure to start at the announced time. I usually also bring this up to remind everyone to keep the time agreement, at least when I work in countries where this is a common understanding on how to relate to time.

When a group of participants arrives late, for example after an exercise in a smaller group, I often bring this up again. As a leader I want to help to create clarity around how to deal with agreements that affect the work of the group. I want to show that if we keep agreements or not, it affects our common results. If we have agreed on certain things and later do not keep them, trust is affected. To talk about issues such as this early on can help us create a culture where we jointly meet the needs of clarity and safety, which are very central in an "immature" group.

To be "on time" or not is also very much culture related, but none the less, it is an issue that can be discussed and a decision around it agreed upon by the group.

Another agreement around time is that I, as the leader, start at the set time with anyone that is there in the room. The most important part here is not to be strict on time, but how to create a group that learns about interdependence.

If I, as a leader, express frustration about the agreements around times not being kept, I want to do so in a way that creates more trust, not less. It is very significant that I do it without the intention to punish, shame or blame anyone who arrives later than agreed upon. If I blame or otherwise punish anyone who arrives late, agreements on time may be kept in the future, but it may be paid for in terms of reduced goodwill towards me as a leader. People keeping time to avoid shame or guilt might make them punctual, but they may see you also as someone that is taking away the joy of getting together. And I believe (from experience but not backed up by any research I can point to) that if a person feels shame for being late it increases the risk of them being late again or actually never showing up again.

In some cultures, to be punctual is significantly more charged than in others. What I am concerned about is not keeping the exact time, but how as a group, we create and apply common agreements that support us in achieving our objectives. In some cultures there are other things that are more loaded, for example how to greet and treat elders or those regarded as our superiors.

Agreements that team members have been involved in forming are in my experience much better kept than decisions that the leader has made alone. So the first thing I do as the leader of a group where people come later than we have decided, is to ask myself if I have checked with them, whether they have agreed with me about times and if they feel they have had any influence on this. Often leaders conclude that just because a schedule has been set people have agreed to it.

Discussions on time are fruitful as long as you do not mix it in with demands, or with ideas of "high morals." If you focus the discussions on interdependency and interconnectedness people will learn important ideas about functioning in cooperation with others.

The Leader can Interrupt

I interrupt, at least in an immature group, if someone takes a lot of time telling personal stories before we have actually connected. When I as a leader interrupt to contribute to the group, I am showing that I want us to focus on certain common things and that I want to help the group to reach its goals. Of course it can also feel uncomfortable for the person I interrupt so I try to do it with care and expressing my concerns of how it is for this person. I also take the chance to point out my motives, to reach the common goal.

Interrupting in a way that builds relationships contributes to greater security and trust in the leader - at least if the interruption is done with respect for the speaker and in a way that maintains connection with that person as well. It is especially valuable for the leader to step in when the group is in the inclusion phase, because it can be challenging to do so for the participants. Although they are participants, they don't yet know if the group has accepted them. If someone is willing to stick his or her neck out and interrupt someone who is talking longer than is supportive, the leader can support both the person in communicating his or her point, while at the same time be there for the person who was interrupted.

Being a leader sometimes means daring to be uncomfortable if that is what is needed to serve the needs of the group. It can sometimes be a challenge to give the group what it needs, which is not necessarily what it asks for, as you might not earn any extra popularity scores while doing it.

If you want certain things to happen in a group, you have every chance to influence it by being a role model. See more about interrupting under the heading "When someone is talking longer than you want to listen" in Chapter 4.

The Openhearted Leader

If someone has been sitting quietly and said nothing for a while I sometimes directly address that person and ask if she or he wants to say something. To express specific requests where I invite people for more active participation can help the group quickly to get everyone into the "boat."

It can provide clarity about what all the participants value and want to achieve by being there. In the inclusion phase of belonging, as a leader I am more than otherwise careful in expressing my requests so that they are concrete and achievable. I do not ask, "What do you feel like doing?" or "What do you want?" as they are difficult questions to answer, especially in an immature group.

At this point I might instead express a suggestion or request that is based on NVC:

I want to do this (describe what, when and how), why (what needs I hope it will be met) is there anything else that needs to be done before or can we start? (A concrete doable request)

It might sound something like this:

I would like everyone to take one of the paper exercises from the middle and spend 10 minutes filling in information about your own examples. Why I suggest that we start this way is so that everyone will have a chance for personal reflection and that we all can learn from each other at a later point.

I'm holding my suggestion as a choice and if there are requests of focusing on something else I might consider that. But I do not expect any protest at this point, as the most important thing for the participants in the belonging phase is not so much on what we are doing. The attention of the participants is focused on if they belong to the group or not.

Most people find it helpful to start with something that can help us connect with each other. I am open to other options and am willing to let my proposal go if it seems more likely that another proposal will better meet the needs of belonging, safety and connection.

Openness in a leader is an invaluable tool in many situations. But in a group where people are focused on exploring whether they want to be included in the group, I do not share very much information about what is going on inside me. I've seen examples of it becoming difficult for some people to feel safe when the leader is revealing feelings that people are not accustomed to see in a leader so early on. If I as a leader am experiencing strong emotions, it will of course be noticed in the group and then it creates more security if I can put on feeling into words. So I express what is going on inside me if I think it will help to meet the needs of security and connection in the group and to adjust to how the situation is.

Willingness to openly express what I feel and take responsibility by connecting my feelings to my needs is one of the most useful tools I have as a leader. This openness about my own needs, together with a focus on listening to other people's reactions with empathy, have often contributed to greater confidence and clarity in my ways of leading a group. To openly dare to show what is going on inside of me as the leader of a group that has matured into the control phase can really help the group forward. In these situations, the leader becomes a model for transparency that can help the group to move into greater cooperation.

In some groups the inclusion phase may be completed within ten minutes (at least for the specific kind of task that the group has to solve), so be prepared to change the way you lead at any time. If you do not, you slow down the development of the group, which in the end could cost you your leadership. It might also mean that the group will never reach its goals.

Evaluate Your Leadership in The Inclusion Phase

In order to evaluate how my leadership has contributed to a group in the inclusion phase I ask myself the following questions:
- Have I given the group members time and opportunity to show themselves?
- Have I have seen and welcomed everyone?
- Have I clarified the common goal(s) for the group?
- Have I given them enough structure so that they can relax and focus on their membership in the group?

Leadership in the Control Phase

In the control phase the leadership is all about supervising the group to help the participants stay on track (or to get back on track when they have lost it). It is also about slowly giving the group more complex tasks so that they may use and demonstrate their skills. Here the leader needs the skill to move in and out of the group in order to see what is going on and to help manage conflict when necessary.

Using NVC as a Leader in the Control Phase

Studying group theories to understand how they work was a relief for me in my role as a leader. I understood why conflicts arose in the groups I participated in or led. Before I accepted that conflicts were a natural part of a group process, I often took responsibility for the conflicts when I was the leader of the group. When I became self-critical I was of much less use, because the focus was on myself and not on what the group needed. I was exhausted and sometimes the hopelessness became so great that I did not want to take on a leadership role any more. It became easier when I, through FIRO and other theories on relationships and groups, got a map to use as support. It described the natural progression in a group. Now I could both grasp what happened in the group and act in a way that benefited the group I was leading - as well as myself. Now it's much clearer to me how I can use my leadership to serve groups. And even more importantly, I can easily decide what I have the power to change and what I do not have the power to change. In this way the knowledge of groups for me has been particularly valuable when groups are in the control phase. Being attentive to the first signs that a person in the group has shifted their focus from gaining clarity around belonging and acceptance, to trying to find clarity around how to use their competence to influence the group, helps me understand what I as a leader can do for the group to help it get the support it needs. The signs I'm talking about are everything from my own feelings, to what people in the group say or do.

People often hesitate to express themselves with honest vulnerability even if that would support them and the group. To support them create trust that they can be understood and heard. One way to do that is early on in the group invite the group members to practice expressing honesty about what is going on within them and to listen to others. Ask them to listen with empathy even when they do not have the same opinions or want the same thing as the person they are listening to. It will support greater openness in the group also in the control phase if they have learnt these skills.

In the control phase it might be helpful to ask them to repeat what they have heard someone else say as it may be a challenge. It usually helps create connection and clarity on how to go further.

Another thing I do is to ask someone to rephrase what they have said in a way that will make it easier for others to hear. It might be when someone labels someone else, instead of saying what he or she actually needs and wants. I might also act as a third party and mediate when it is needed, mostly without calling it mediation.[2]

When the group has reached this phase I sometimes use exercises on how we can express ourselves with "Classic NVC." It reminds them that the way they express themselves can have a big impact. It is useful to remind the group of this if things heat up and they want to maintain connection with each other. I have every chance to be a role model here by using my own skills in communication.

If I believe that it contributes to clarity in certain situations in a group I stick to classical NVC. This is especially useful in a group that has as their common objective to study NVC. I am careful to communicate with the help of all the components and show how mutual listening with empathy can create connection and clarity.

In the control phase I participate more actively than before as a leader. I consciously choose to express what is going on in me more frequently than I did in the inclusion phase. At this point I change the leadership style I was using at the start, which was based on creating structure and security, to a more mentoring leadership. As well as listening to what is going on within the group participants, I also honestly express my own feelings, needs and desires. An important tool here is vulnerable openness from me as a leader. It is very helpful for the group here if the leader is willing to participate in discussions and maybe even in exercises.

The experience in a group focused on finding roles is that of in-dependency. People are ready to take pretty big risks that could

---

2. Read more about how mediation with the help of NVC in A Helping Hand, Mediation with Nonviolent Communication by Liv Larsson Friare Liv. 2010.

even lead to exclusion. With the help of NVC I take every chance I see to make them aware of the ways in which they are interdependent to each other. When they understand this, it is usually easier for them to be vulnerable about what they want in a way that does not demonstrate independence, but leads the group forward. Although I have not seen anyone try to teach NVC by direct competitive exercises or contests, let me mention that this is a phase where competition seems particularly inhibitory to a group's development.

Precisely for this reason it is important to pay attention to how to instruct, inform and who to ask for support from in the group. In the control phase the participants of a group easily feel that the leader "favors" one or another and it may contribute to increased distance and sense of competition. To give the group tasks where they need to work together in order to arrive at a solution is an effective way to support the group. The exercise "Basic Empathy Skills" on page 88 is an example of such an exercise.

To minimize competition thinking I avoid using words such as teams (which is easily understood to be about competition) and instead, ask them to "form smaller groups" (which is more easily perceived as if it's about cooperation). I could say, "arrived at the best idea for a solution "(which can easily be perceived as encouraging competition) but if I want to minimize the competition, I can say something like:

Think about how to approach this person to create connection. I am dividing you into groups to make it easier for you to talk about this dilemma. I would like you to find some suggestions on how to connect with this person that we can try out together afterwards.

A seemingly small thing such as asking different people in the group for help with practical things decreases the risks of someone being regarded as your "favorite." It will help the group see that you are all working towards the same common goals.

If you need help with a specific thing where certain knowledge is needed, this is different. Then you can openly express why you are asking a specific person for help.

I am asking Frida as I know that she has been working with this type of software before and I am confident that I can leave this task with her right now.

The above comments may sound trite, but when participants in a group focus on issues of competence and power it can make a big difference how the leader uses words. NVC has given me tools that I have used many times to turn questioning about my leadership to the advantage for the group. Using NVC, it is possible to transform what we hear as criticism as a benchmark for whether we are truly serving the group in a maximum way.

If someone, for example, would say:

But do you really have the skills to lead this group, do you have enough knowledge needed?

I can meet it with empathy and say something like:

Is it so that when you see how I respond to X you are worried because you like it when people treat each other with care and respect?

If their answer is yes, you can either clarify your motives in acting as you did, tell them more about your needs behind what you have suggested, or ask them if they have any ideas about how it could be done differently. Make sure you do not listen with empathy to make them shut up or to cover a mistake you made. Listen with empathy because you want to connect and to learn more about how everyone's needs can be met.

Since I've learned that behind everything people say there are needs that we all share, I listen and really take in what they are saying. I have the intention to monitor the questioning as an aid to protect needs and values, even when it has been said in a way that makes it a challenge to hear it. What otherwise could be heard as criticism can now become energy for both the group and me.

Handling Conflicts

When conflicts arise in a group during the control phase, as a leader I often try to help the participants handle the conflict, or mediate, if necessary. I can also point out conflicts I think I see between members of the group that are not being openly talked about. If I do that, I make sure I connect what I say with a clear observation. It could be, for example:

When I notice that we have used more than 40 minutes to come to a decision on this, I wonder if there is something we have missed. I would like to hear from some of you as to what you feel and need in relation to this fact that it has taken us so long. Is there anyone who is willing to share something about this?

Or more directly:
This is the fourth time I have heard you making a new proposal just after Maria has proposed something. I am curious to hear if you are willing to say something about what is going on in you in relationship to Maria?

When I phrase the question more directly I make myself ready for more of the conflict to come up on the table. When someone questions me or the goals of the group, I as the leader have an opportunity to show what I value. I can show how I cherish relationships, that people are listening to each other, and that we have accepted many different thoughts and perspectives. Depending on how I respond to protests and issues that I perceive as provocative, I give different signals. By stopping to listen to what they have to say I show that I appreciate that they are reflecting on what is going on, rather than just obeying orders and adapting. All doubts can thus contribute to the group's development. My focus as a leader in the control phase is to:

- Facilitate relationships between the group and me.

- Increase the motivation of the group to work towards our common goals.

- Encourage distributed responsibility among all of us.
- Emphasize that they can get along without me. Create independence in relation to the leader.
- Suggest methods that reduce tension between the leader and group and increase tension between the group and its mission and goals.
- Continually clarify how individual and team goals go together.
- Identify and highlight members' resources, competence and skills so that they will most benefit the group.

When you encounter an existing group (for example a working group) in order to help them to manage a conflict, there are some certain dilemmas to watch out for. If you are hired by, for example, the supervisor of a work group, you will probably be seen as his or her extended arm, even if you say you are there to listen to all parties. It may take some time to gain their trust. When a working group is involved in choosing who will come to help or mediate in a conflict and they choose you, it is usually easier for them to open up.

For most groups if the boss, teacher or any other person in authority is participating the situation will be different than if they do not participate. In these situations, be aware of whether the impact of the boss's participation means that certain things are not being expressed openly or are hidden away.

Evaluating Your Leadership in The Control Phase

The questions I ask myself to evaluate how my leadership has contributed to a group in the phase can be:
- Have I given the group enough space to explore issues about impact, power and leadership?

- Have I reminded them of the goals of the group?
- Have I shared enough about what is going on inside me, so that focus does not end up with the participants trying to guess about this?
- Have I drawn attention to the conflicts they may need support to handle?
- Have I given them enough structure for them to feel safe to focus on membership in the group?
- Have I done anything that might increase competition?
- Have I given them small or big enough challenges?
- Have I helped them move from the experience of being independent to ensure that they are mutually dependent?

Leadership in Openness Phase

The leadership style when the group has matured into the openness phase is based on the attitude that we are all mutually dependent. I show that I accept individual decisions if its clear that people take responsibility of how this affects the group.

The focus is about supporting the group to become as self-sustaining as possible without losing direction and momentum. While I am willing to let the group take more responsibility, I show that I am available if anyone needs me. Questions or doubts about the group's direction, I take as an opportunity to fine-tune where we are heading and how we can achieve our goals.

Using NVC As a Leader (Openness Phase)

Studying NVC we can attach great importance to mutual dependency and care within the group. Sometimes I have seen students in groups studying NVC lose care for their surroundings because the participants have become so preoccupied with the meaningfulness of looking further into this mode of communication. If I see these signs in a group I am supervising (for example that they are not cleaning up after themselves in common snack facilities because they have become so absorbed in talking about something), I remind them of the beauty in considering also the needs of others. It can be a great start to a conversation that can expand the group's perspective and open up their awareness of other people's needs. My aim in this phase is primarily to:

- Give each person space to express his or her needs, dreams and requests.

- Make everyone in the group more aware of the resources, experience and knowledge the group has and to use them where they best fit.

- Delegate leadership to the person who in the moment seems most suited to lead.

- Point out the signs I see of our interdependency in the group and explain how this interdependence enhances our ability to achieve our goal.

- Make observations of how we are interdependent even with people outside the group and to explain how taking this in consideration enhances our ability to achieve our goal.

- Clarify and work to reach the group's goals and objectives.

Evaluating Your Leadership in The Openness Phase

The questions I ask myself in evaluating how my leadership has contributed to a group in the openness phase may include:
- Have I "stepped aside," observed, and allowed the group participants to handle things on their own?
- Have I reminded the group enough of the common goals?
- Have I given them the chance to support each other as well as me?

- Have I created new stimulating challenges for the group?
- Am I missing some important issues around value that the group is avoiding?

Intermediate Stages

In addition to the three main phases (Inclusion, control, openness) groups sometimes experience periods of transition or rest. Both are characterized by the absence of conflicts. They are known as the comfort phase and the idyll phase. They can sometimes be difficult to distinguish and are more important in some groups.

The Comfort Phase

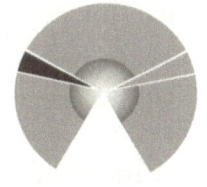

Before a team goes into the control phase they often pass something called the comfort phase. The group goes into this phase when they have solved the last question about membership and when everyone feels that they have a place in the group. During the inclusion phase conflicts are avoided and questions about leadership and other matters of power and responsibility may have been experienced as too challenging to get to a grip on.

Also characteristic of this phase are expressions such as "This is such a great group of wonderful people," "We are so similar and have no conflicts," or "I have never been part of such a fantastic group of people." In this phase people rest and collect strength before going on to handling the conflicts that still exist within the group.

The Idyll Phase

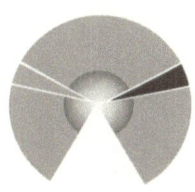

This phase comes after the control phase and is generally preceded by an intense conflict between members or a crisis in the group. Usually the conflicts involve issues of leadership, power, responsibility and influence. People experience freedom, relief, hope and joy, having succeeded in dealing with difficult issues and perhaps challenging confrontations. If you have experienced this within a group once, you'll probably recognize it the next time. It is a great relief to get to this rest stop, and in this phase many experience euphoria, deep connection and relief.

A deeper group identity and belonging has developed now and everyone better understands and accepts their role in the group. The difficulties in this phase is that the group does not tend to continue to work effectively to achieve their goals but instead expends a lot of energy into preserving this great relationship.

If they stay here after the much-needed rest, the leader may need to help them out of this zone, for example by expressing requests in relation to their common goals. Sometimes, it mean that questions around roles and skills, and about who will be allowed to influence the group will come up again if they have not been fully worked out. This might seem as a step back, but it is actually deepening the group's maturity and readiness for the next phase, the openness phase.

The members of the group:
- begin to identify the conflicts using more straight forward and honest language.
- show greater willingness to find solutions to conflicts and hence to change their own opinions and positions,
- allocate leadership, roles and responsibility within the group based on an objective discussion of the individual's competence,
- develop a group identity and understand their roles within the group.

The Leader Helps the Group to Develop

At various times, the leader can ask different questions to find out valuable information

Critical points in the inclusion phase:
- Are the membership issues resolved? Is everyone in the boat?
- Has everybody taken part? Is everyone allowed in?
- Has the group got stuck where it feels comfortable, but where movement towards the common goals has stopped?

Critical points in the control phase:
- Is the leader having the impact he or she needs and wants?
- Are the participants getting the impact they want?
- Are uncertainties about the role of the leader standing in the way of team development?
- Which conflicts have not yet been handled?
- How are differences being managed?
- Which responsibility issues are still not being handled?

Critical points in the comfort phase:
- Has the group got stuck in the comfort phase, where it feels comfortable to be, but where little development is taking place?
- Are the set goals helping the team forward? Are there enough challenges and inspiration?

When The Group is In The Phase of Comfort

Even the leader needs to rest and this is a good time to pause for reflection. Now the group is soon ready for bigger challenges and when the group has gathered its energy, the leader will show where these challenges exist. Give it some time.

When The Group is in Idyll Phase

The group will stop here for a while to celebrate that they have successfully gone through some major conflicts. After a much needed rest, the leader helps the group to mature by pointing toward the goal again. Sometimes it leads to the group returning to the control phase and the role of the leader being examined and questioned in order to further clarify it. Then the group is ready to go on to the openness phase.

Natural or Cultural

Over the more than thirty years that I have used FIRO to understand and describe what happens in groups, I have often wondered if there is something that could be called a natural group process, which exists because of cultural origin? Which of the behaviors that I have described during the different phases would occur in other cultures than a traditional hierarchical one? Do groups - that do not exist in domination cultures based on judgments about what is right or wrong, and normal or abnormal - develop in other ways? Are there any group behaviors that are natural for all of us humans and that are common to all cultures?

One dilemma is that most research on group development has been made on people who have grown up in cultures of a certain kind. This of course affects the perspective we use in looking at what is happening. And this makes it difficult to distinguish between what is natural humanity and what is culturally learned.

Just as with the horses mentioned earlier, people in groups go through different maturation processes and dimensions as the FIRO theory describes, and I think the origin, the core of all our behaviors in a group are intended to benefit group.

It may be that some theories about groups are of greater use in cultures that are built on domination thinking. If for no other reason, than because theories are useful as they give some kind of map of the often confusing domination jungle that we can follow until we find our own way. Perhaps theories are useful because many of us that are brought up in a domination system have lost our natural ways to cooperate. The important thing for me is that we use FIRO - theory, (as well as all other theories), in a way that contributes to greater respect, deeper cooperation and more life-serving ways of living and relating.

When Theories are Used as Weapons

One of my dilemmas with FIRO theory is that the maturity of the group is described in analytical terms, rather than observing what is going on in the present. Using the tools of NVC I have realized how valuable it is to base communication on observations and not on analysis or judgments.

Therefore, I am careful with how I use analyzes anyone makes of a group with the help of FIRO theory and remind myself that they are nothing but analyzes.

A few times I heard people in groups where FIRO has been presented, use the theory to criticize someone they are annoyed with:
You are just in the control phase now. Let go!

I have heard people abdicate responsibility by saying something in the line of:
Since the group was in the control phase, nobody listened to me. There was nothing I could do.

I mourn every time I hear things such as in the above examples. I am sorry to find that something that could serve a team is now used in a manner that obstructs the development of it. Just as many undergo a period in which they act as "NVC police" (who comment on what they think is the wrong way to express oneself), we can use the FIRO-theory in a way that makes it difficult to co-operate, instead of supporting it.

When I introduce the FIRO theory, I usually ask the participants to regard it as a map of a city. A city is being rebuilt or repaired all the time; still you can find your way with the help of a map, as long as it is updated. But sometimes, however, a road has been rebuilt and has become a dead end, a building has been built where we thought there was a football field, so we no longer get support from the map in finding our way towards the goal. My hope is that we can use theories as a means to find new places and that if it no longer does that, we are better off letting it go.

Teambuilding

NVC training in a workplace can almost always help to strengthen ways of collaboration and communication within groups. This, however, sometimes takes time to notice, as often the first thing to happen is that hidden conflicts rise to the surface. At first this makes it appear that collaboration has worsened, when what has actually happened is that major housecleaning has been done.

I am sometimes invited to share NVC at a workplace in order to strengthen a team. The organizers may be hoping that new insights about communication skills gained in a few hours of training will increase group cooperation and communication. However, I usually say that I cannot promise this kind of improvement after only one day of training, even if some communication skills may be improved.

If team building is what the group wants and needs, there are many ways to do it and working on communication skills is often only one of the things that need to be worked on.

Talking About The Group Process

Does the group function in a way that leads towards the goals of the group? If not - what can be changed?

These two questions can be used as support to see where your leadership needs to be used. In order to be able to answer the questions, the goals of the team needs to be clear. It is the group that does the job, but you can help it forward by having a conversation with group members about how the group works together by using the questions below.

No single person will carry the whole "truth" about a group and the aim is not to identify how something "is." The purpose is to ascertain whether you want to change something in order to make it easier to everyone's needs so they can be met whenever possible.

Questions to use to create participation in the group process:

- Does everyone have space in the group in ways they wish and need?
- Do the participants work effectively to achieve their goals?
- Are differences accepted in a way that everyone thinks is okay?
- Are there any needs that are not being met in the group?
- Are there any needs that seem to have "priority" over others?
- Are there any unspoken "rules" about how to behave in this group?
- What prevents the group from functioning optimally in order to achieve the objectives?
- What expressions of dissent are expressed in the group?
- What is the conflicts about?
- Is there anything you would like to change in your cooperation? Communication?

FAQ on Groups & Leadership

Is it possible to meet everyone's needs without getting stuck?
In some groups, members consciously or unconsciously avoid themes or subjects. If these subjects are important for achieving the goals of the team it is fruitful if the leader can bring them up to discussion. The group members might need to talk about the situation in order to find ways to take everyones needs in consideration. It does not mean that we stay in the discussion about it forever as this might also get in the way of people having their needs met. We stay with the topic as long as we predict it will meet more needs than if we would let go of it.

The opposite can come true as well. In some groups the best support for the group is if the leader reminds them of their common goal, and asks them to act instead of continuing with processing or discussion at a certain point. It is sometimes quite uncomfortable to express these types of requests to a group that has spent much time dealing with a conflict by talking, but it might be the best support you can give.

I don't focus on satisfying all needs at all times. I instead focus on listening to people and the needs they express, allowing myself to be influenced by what I hear. Listening and paying attention to needs is one step closer to meeting them.

When is a group too large to meet everyone's needs?
Whether the needs of everyone can be met or not, does not depend on the size of the group. It is not only leaders that can satisfy needs. The leader can aim to meet the needs of everyone but whether needs are met or not depends on more than that.

A leader may help a big group with meeting individuals needs, for example the need to be seen or heard, through dividing the group into smaller groups. To meet the needs of the community in a big group, we can, for example, make use of games, music and other things that may engage many people simultaneously. I am not responsible for others' needs being met, not even when I'm the formal leader of a group, but I have a possibility to meet my needs of contribution through doing that.

Need there be a willingness to learn NVC?

I sometimes lead introductions of one to three hours for groups of people who have not used NVC on their own, such as in workplace groups. When I am going to lead an NVC training that is longer than that, I want the participants to be able to choose not to participate without it having any impact on their salary or some other negative effect. If people do not experience their participation as voluntary it may be difficult to talk about freedom of choice and autonomy, which are such important parts of NVC. Read more about this under the question, "When people do not experience their participation as voluntary."

What Happens If The Leader is More Open Than The Group?

What happens in a group if the leader is more open than the group depends entirely on which development phase the group is in. When the group is new (in the inclusion phase) the leader who openly shows emotions sometimes can slow the group process down. The group may quickly open up to talk about feelings but many times there will be some sort of backlash after some time. Similarly, a leader who does not choose to be open about what she or he feels, when the group has developed (to the control phase) is slowing down the groups maturation. A lot of energy can be spent on thinking about what is going on within the leader and thereby the group becomes less effective and may have difficulties in achieving their goals.

What Happens When a Group Gets A More Difficult Task Than It is Ready For?

There are many things that can happen when a group gets a bigger and more challenging task than the group participants are ready for. The first is that the group may dissolve because the pressure becomes too great. But if the challenge is not large enough, the group participants may jointly mobilize strength and use their resources to cope. When this happens, the group participants often experience pride and old conflicts are sometimes simultaneously resolved.

Good luck!

Since I started sharing my understanding of NVC many different tools have appeared on the market to make it easier. I and other authors have written books on a number of themes to show that NVC can be used in many different settings and relationships. Card games have been developed to deepen the understanding that NVC can give us in gaining new perspective on human connection. Different structures to deal with mediation, restore trust and reconcile conflict have been tested and enjoyed.

This book is one of my attempts to send forward what I have received, tested and have successfully used. I hope it will support you as a reader to dare to try to share what you understand about communication. I hope you will create spaces for people to learn and explore human connection, and in turn give this forward in any way you find the most joy in. Good luck!

Appendix

Key Differentiations - Keys To Deepen Connection and Understanding

Gaining Clarity

In learning a new concept, it is helpful to distinguish it from related concepts. There are a number of key differentiations that can help us understand more about NVC and the possibilities it opens.[1]

Exploring the differences between concepts can lead to new discoveries about the way you communicate. It can also sharpen your ability to share NVC with others. When you are clear about the following key differentiations you can draw upon that clarity to answer questions from students or others who are wondering about any aspect of NVC. If someone, for example, asks what you really mean by empathy, it might be easier to explain it if you describe in what way empathy differs from sympathy. Not as if one is better than the other, just that there is a difference between them and that we can choose the one that creates connection in any given situation.

The key differentiations below can also be used as a foundation in a presentation of NVC. If you have an hour-long presentation, your might aim at clarifying only one or a few of the key differentiations. For example you could focus on how to distinguish between observations and interpretations (Key differentiation 8 on the list below). Before you answer questions by using key differentiations, make sure that the person asking really wants information and that the question or protest is not an expression of a need for empathy.

If you want to communicate that you are most concerned with connecting, respond to questions with an empathy guess but also following it up with a clarifying theoretical answer.

---

[1]. To be able to describe key differentiations of NVC is part of the process of becoming a certified trainer by CNVC. www.cnvc.org

Key Differentiations:

1. "Being" giraffe versus "doing" giraffe.
2. Giraffe honesty versus jackal honesty.
3. Empathy versus sympathy.
4. Protective versus punitive use of force.
5. Power with versus power over.
6. Appreciation versus approval, compliments and praise.
7. Choice versus submission or rebellion.
8. Observations versus observations mixed with evaluation.
9. Feelings versus feelings mixed with judgments.
10. Needs versus requests.
11. Requests versus demands.
12. Stimulus versus cause.
13. Moralistic judgments versus value judgments.
14. Natural versus habitual.
15. Interdependence versus dependence or independence.
16. Life-connected versus life-alienated.
17. Compromise versus shift.
18. Persisting versus demanding.
19. Obedience versus self-discipline.
20. Fear of authority versus respect for authority.
21. Vulnerability versus weakness.
22. Love as a feeling versus love as a need.
23. Self-Empathy versus acting out, repressing, or wallowing in feelings.
24. Idiomatic versus classical (formal) Giraffe
25. Empathic sensing versus intellectual guessing
26. Guessing versus knowing.
27. Screaming in jackal versus screaming in giraffe.
28. Receiving no from a jackal versus no from a giraffe.

Key Differentiations

Below are attempts to describe some key differentiations with a few words. They are in no way comprehensive explanations, but will hopefully stimulate your curiosity to explore how they affect your ability to communicate and how you can use them when you share NVC. If you want to get an extensive overview go to the book by Katarina Hoffmann and myself called *Cracking the Communication Code*.

	The Difference between	
1	"Being" Giraffe - To have the attitude of living with compassion and honesty	"Doing" Giraffe - Making use of the strategies NVC is based on, and using different strategies that can support it, without necessarily having the intention to create connection.
2	Giraffe Honesty - Honesty is based on observations, feelings, needs and requests. Expressing oneself in order to create connection.	Jackal Honesty - Honesty is based on moralistic judgments about what someone is. Expressing oneself in order to be heard.
3	Empathy - My attention is on somebody's feelings and needs.	Sympathy - My attention is on my own reaction to what I see or hear.
4	Protective use of force - I focus on protecting and meeting needs. Trying to influence behavior in order to meet needs.	Punitive use of force - I focus on what the other person does, what is right or wrong, and punish misconduct.

The Difference between	
5	Power with - We use our power to involve everyone's resources and energy. Everyone's needs are important. As far as possible decisions are made jointly.	Power over - One person or group controls everyone else. Decisions are made without being connected to the needs of everyone.
6	Appreciation - Based on an evaluation of how an action has met needs and is creating pleasant feelings.	Praise, approval, compliments - Based on assessments of how you are when you are right or normal. Correct behavior is approved of.
7	Choice - Actions coming from internal motivation. Focused on how needs of others and my own needs can be met.	Rebellion or submission - Actions being controlled by external motivation without any direct connection with needs.
8	Observation - What we perceive with our senses. Describes what we see, hear, feel, smell, taste without interpreting it as good, bad, normal and so on.	Observations mixed with judgments - What we think about our sense of perceptions. Our intellectual understanding of what is happening according to our senses.

	The Difference between	
9	Feeling - Experienced in the body. A reaction to needs being met or not. ("I feel scared")	Feeling mixed with thoughts - Interpretations of what is happening in the body mixed with information of what happened when that feeling occurred. ("I feel attacked")
10	Needs - General, abstract forces. Something we truly value and want to protect.	Requests/Strategies - Concrete, specific actions with the intention to meet needs.
11	Requests - If the answer to a request becomes negative, I continue the dialog in order to eventually find a new strategy.	Demands - When the answer is "no," punishments or threats are used to show that the "no" is not accepted.
12	Stimulus - Something that stimulates a reaction but does not cause it.	Cause - makes needs and values the explanation of the feeling. Without the root cause no feeling occurs.
13	Value judgments - Judgments are based on whether something is in line with what I value and not.	Moralistic judgments - Judgments are based on ideas about what is right and wrong or good and bad.
14	Natural - actions and thoughts based on what we are born with.	Habitual - We do something because it is a habit of ours to do so or have seen someone else doing it for so long that it seems natural.

		The Difference between	
	15	Interdependence - Everything we do affects others. Everything others do affects us.	Dependence or independence - I cannot do anything without the okay of others / I can do whatever I want to and it does not matter what others think.
	16	Life-connected - The attention is focused on what can meet needs, both mine and others.	Life-alienated - Focused on moral judgments and how we act to maintain a system regardless of how it looks.
	17	Shift Focus: meeting needs. Intention: Find a solution that everyone is satisfied with.	Compromise Focus: To arrive at a solution. Intention: Finding a solution that all can live with, where everyone gives and gets something.
	18	Persisting - Passionate commitment to my own needs. Want to get them met in connection with others without punishment.	Demanding - Passionate commitment to my own needs, but without taking into account the needs of choice and the autonomy of others.
	19	Self-discipline - When I do something it is because I consciously choose to and am prepared to take responsibility for my actions.	Obedience - When I obey I do something because I think it is my duty, that I should or have to do it.

	The Difference between	
20	Respect for authority - I see other people as human with needs and I benefit from the knowledge of others without submitting.	Fear of authority - I do things to avoid punishment or to be rewarded. Focus who or what that can punish and reward.
21	Vulnerability - The vulnerable and honest expression of what I feel and that I have a need for something even if I am sticking out my neck.	Weakness is when I talk of feeling bad, not having enough or not having the power to do something about it.
22	22. Love as a feeling - What do I feel? Expressed in words of feelings.	Love as a need - What do I need? Expressed in words of needs.
23	Wallowing in feelings - Focused on feeling sorry for myself. I relate what I feel to something I cannot control instead of to my needs or values. Turns me into "a victim of circumstances." Repress feelings - Pushing feelings away in all kinds of ways. Acting out. Letting feelings determine how I act. I'm afraid so I decline, angry so I beat.	Self Empathy - My attention is focused on my feelings and needs. I relate what I feel to my needs. Provides me power to act under different circumstances.

	The Difference between	
24	Everyday Giraffe / Idiomatic Giraffe - Focused on what creates connection.	Classical formal Giraffe - Focused on the use of NVC and the 4 components.
25	Emphatic sensing - Intention: To create connection. Focused on the present.	Intellectual guessing - Intent: To achieve connection by understanding. Focused on the past or on other people.
26	Guessing I want to connect and am open to what is happening every moment. Things change.	Claiming to know. I have understood it all. This is how it is.
27	Screaming in "giraffe" - Passionate commitment to my and others' needs. Passionately expresses feelings, needs and desires – maybe in a loud voice to create connection.	Screaming in "jackal" - Crying out judgments that blame and attack.

	The Difference between	
28	No, from a giraffe - Based on needs and on listening to everyone's needs.	No, from a jackal - Based on rules and on what is morally right, wrong, normal, fitting, etc.

List of feeling words

Afraid
Alive
Ambivalent
Angry
Ashamed
Awake
Bored
Calm
Comfortable
Confused
Curious
Delighted
Depressed
Desperate
Disappointed
Disinterested
Downhearted
Embarrassed
Energetic
Enthusiastic
Frustrated
Furious
Gloomy
Grateful
Grumpy
Happy

Hopeful
Impatient
Irritated
Lonely
Moved
Nervous
Overwhelmed
Perplexed
Proud
Restless
Sad
Satisfied
Shocked
Skeptical
Stressed
Sure
Surprised
Suspicious
Tense
Thrilled
Tired
Uncomfortable
Uneasy
Upset
Vulnerable
Worried

List of words for human needs

Acceptance
Acknowledgment
Authenticity
Autonomy
Balance
Beauty
Belonging
Care
Celebration
Choice
Clarity
Closeness
Communication
Community
Connection
Cooperation
Creativity
Ease
Efficiency
Empathy
Equality
Freedom
Fun, Play
Harmony
Health
Honesty
Importance
Inspiration

Integrity
Learning
Light
Love
Meaning
Movement
Mutuality
Nurturance
Order
Participation
Peace
Predictability
Protection
Relaxation
Respect
Rest, sleep
Safety
Sexual expression
Shared reality
Support
To be seen & heard
To contribute
To mourn
Touch
Trust
Understanding
Warmth

Literature and references

Brown Brené, The Gift of imperfection.

Glickstein, Lee (1999) Be Heard Now! Tap into your inner speaker and communicate with ease. Broadway books.

Hartmann, Thom(2001) *The Last Hours of Ancient Sunlight*. Hodder & Stoughton.

Hoffmann & Larsson (2015), *Cracking the Communication Code. Nonviolent Communication by 42 Key Differentiations*. Illustrated by Vilhelm Nilsson. Friare Liv.

Larsson, Liv (2011), A Helping Hand.
- (2012), *Anger, Guilt and Shame. Reclaiming Power and Choice*.
- (2012), *Relationships. Freedom without Distance, Belonging without Control*.
- (2014), *The Power of Gratitude! Friare Liv*.
- (2017) *Human Connection at Work*.

Owen Harrison (1999 *Open Space Technogoly a User's Guide*. Berrett-Koehler Publishers

Rosenberg, Marshall (2015) *Nonviolent Communication, a Language for Life*. Puddle Dancer Press.

Vos & Dryden (2005) *The New Learning Revolution*. Network Educational Press Ltd

The Author - Liv Larsson

Liv Larsson has lead trainings since 1978 with everything from conflict resolution to organizational change and personal development as a focus. Since 1992 in her own company. She is a certified Nonviolent Communication trainer with CNVC with her base in Sweden. Larsson is leading trainings all over the world. She is active as a mediator in different kind of conflicts. One of the organizations where she acts as the mediators is FSC (Forest Stewardship Council) where she mediates conflicts between the indigenous group of Sweden (the Sami) and the forest companies of Sweden. Author of 20 books on communication, conflicts, shame, anger, mediation and much more.

Titles published in English:
- *A Helping Hand, Mediation with NVC*
- *Anger, Guilt & Shame - Reclaiming Power and Choice*
- *Relationships. Freedom without Distance, Connection without Control*
- *Cracking the Communication Code. 42 Key differentiations (Co-autored with Katarina Hoffmann)*
- *The Power of Gratitude*
- *Needbased Eating*
- *Human connection at work*

Find out more about Liv Larsson's work.
www.friareliv.com
www.livlarsson.com

Other books in english by Liv Larsson

Other books in english by Liv Larsson

Read more and order at www.friareliv.com

If you look for swedish books you find them here www.friareliv.se

www.ingramcontent.com/pod-product-compliance
Lightning Source LLC
Chambersburg PA
CBHW032022230426
43671CB00005B/175